About this book

Why is this topic important?

e-Learning represents an extraordinary opportunity for individuals and organizations. With its low-cost delivery, interactive capabilities, and 24/7 global accessibility, it provides convenient and affordable opportunities for skills and career growth. e-Learning can help both individuals and organizations realize more of their potential and gain a better understanding of the world around us. It can lead to success and a happier, more satisfying life.

Unfortunately, much of today's e-learning falls far short of its potential. Instead of assisting learners and blending effectively with other learning aids, it simply throws out overwhelming amounts of information. It fails to adapt to individual learner needs, provide meaningful learning events, and exercise new skills to the point of proficiency.

What can you achieve with this book?

This is the first and foundational book of a forthcoming series of short books that will guide you through the many tasks of creating worthwhile e-learning. Although the tasks are all interrelated, each book focuses on a single component—with the exception of this book. As a foundation, this book provides an overview of the entire process of creating powerful e-learning and it provides details for defining an e-learning project, conducting a Savvy Start, and evaluating iterative application releases.

By applying the techniques presented in this book, all based on decades of award-winning work by pioneers, experts, and leaders in the field of e-learning, you will be able to produce much more effective e-learning applications.

How is this book organized?

There are three parts. The first part includes real-world scenarios that represent the challenges e-learning projects often face. Success in e-learning comes not from dealing with project design and development as an academic exercise, but from recognizing and managing the context and leading the many individuals involved.

The second part reviews problems with typical design processes used and outlines departures needed. An iterative approach, use of rapid prototyping, and involvement of key stakeholders at the right times are keys to today's successful designs.

The third part details the process of iterative design supported by rapid prototyping. It includes an agenda with annotated events to help you conduct dynamic design sessions. A discussion of iterative development, which must be closely coupled with iterative design, defines iterative releases and includes detailed evaluation checklists.

About the library series

After success with Authorware, Inc. and Macromedia, I felt that I had made a contribution to learning that would satisfy me through retirement. And retire Mary Ann and I did . . . for a few months.

But as my colleagues and I observed what happened with tools that made development of interactive learning systems so much easier to master, it was clear the job wasn't done. Instead of wondrously varied instructional paradigms burgeoning forth, offering more learning fun and effectiveness to the benefit of people and organizations everywhere, we found dry, boring, pedantic presentation of content followed by posttests. The very model of instruction that was drudgery without technology was being replicated and inflicted on ever greater numbers of captive audiences.

Making technology easier to use provided the means, but not the guidance necessary to use it well. To atone for this gross oversight on my part, I formed Allen Interactions in 1993 with a few of my closest and most talented friends in e-learning. Our mission was and is to help everyone and anyone produce better technology-enhanced learning experiences. We established multiple studios within our company so that these teams of artisans could build long-term relationships with each other and their clients. Studios develop great internal efficiencies and, most importantly, get to understand their clients' organizations and performance needs intimately—sometimes better than clients understand them themselves.

Although our studios compete in the custom development arena, we also share our best practices openly and freely. We hope our award-winning applications will serve as models for others to emulate. We teach and mentor in-house organizations who aspire to create great learning applications. And, in close association with the American Society for Training & Development (ASTD), we offer certificate programs to help others develop effective design and development skills.

This series of books is yet another way we are doing our best to help advance the field of technology-enhanced learning. I've not intentionally held back any secrets in putting forth the best practices our studios are continually enhancing.

This, the first book in the series, presents the foundational process of successive approximation. Six books are planned for this library, each to be focused on one major aspect of the process of designing and developing great e-learning applications. I plan to address instructional design, project management, deployment, and more. When the series is compiled, I hope it will be a useful tool for developing great and valuable learning experiences.

Michael Allen's e-Learning Library

Creating Successful e-Learning
A Rapid System for Getting It Right First Time, Every Time

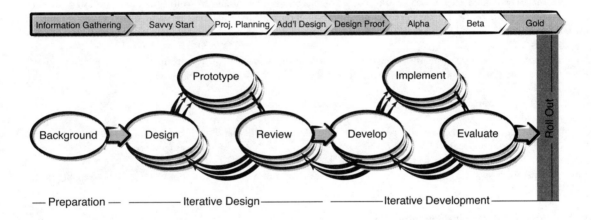

Michael W. Allen

Pfeiffer
A Wiley Imprint
www.pfeiffer.com

Published by Pfeiffer
An Imprint of Wiley
989 Market Street, San Francisco, CA 94103-1741
www.pfeiffer.com

For additional copies/bulk purchases of this book in the U.S. please contact 800-274-4434.

Pfeiffer books and products are available through most bookstores. To contact Pfeiffer directly call our Customer Care Department within the U.S. at 800-274-4434, outside the U.S. at 317-572-3985, fax 317-572-4002, or visit www.pfeiffer.com.

Pfeiffer also publishes its books in a variety of electronic formats. Some content that appears in print may not be available in electronic books.

Library of Congress Cataloging-in-Publication Data

Allen, Michael W.,
  Creating successful e-learning : a rapid system for getting it right first time,
  every time / Michael W. Allen.
      p. cm.
  Includes bibliographical references and index.
  ISBN-13: 978-0-7879-8300-0 (pbk.)
  ISBN-10: 0-7879-8300-4 (pbk.)
  1. Employees—Training of—Computer-assisted instruction. 2. Instructional systems—Design. I. Title.
  HF5549.5.T7A4685 2006
  658.3'1240785—dc22   2006004172

Printed in the United States of America

Printing 10 9 8 7 6 5 4 3 2 1

Cover Photo of Michael Allen by Courtney Platt, Grand Cayman B.W.I.

Contents

For Martin Lipshutz, my friend, partner, and mentor.

Acknowledgments

There are many more people than I can possibly list here that deserve and have my appreciation for helping discover and define successive approximation, teaching me what I think I know about learning and instruction, and helping me prepare this book. I hope they have no doubt about my gratitude.

Of particular and indispensable aid in producing this book were Len Eichten, Ethan Edwards, Patrick Krekelberg, Ted Manning, Mindy Powell, Shane Reese, Richard Sites, Laurie Squillace, all of the amazing e-learning studios at Allen Interactions who provided materials, examples, and much needed constructive criticism. Detailed critique from Will Thalheimer, president and principal researcher at Work-Learning Research, was invaluable. Input from Dale Hommes, Benjamin Kitt, Martin Lipshutz, Paul Nickelson, John Welsh, and Jason Zeaman of Allen Interactions provided a wealth of good ideas and inspiration.

My dearest Mary Ann proofread tirelessly through the iterative process, while our son, Christopher, laid out the book and made countless revisions with the patience and enthusiasm of a seasoned successive approximation developer.

Preface

As a student, I've had some great experiences and plenty of awful ones too. My best teachers imparted their passion for learning by sharing what their knowledge and skill had done for them. You could feel their sheer delight in knowing and understanding things.

Richard Simpson was the best of the best. Teaching business and leadership subjects in our small Iowa high school, Mr. Simpson consistently broke school rules, giving hall passes, for example, to pretty much anyone who wanted them. Almost no one took advantage of his flexibility because he cared about us. Using his passes, we escaped study hall, with its absolute silence, stay in your seat dicta. We spent that time in his classrooms that were filled with work tables and office equipment we could use for projects of our own choosing. We formed study groups and talked *out loud*. We were active and we were learning. My career goal is to continue the excellent work he did to create beneficial learning experiences.

Through technology, we can reach so many people. If we do it well, many benefit. If we do it poorly, we waste the time of many and perhaps sacrifice the one opportunity some will ever encounter to learn something of unexpected importance to their lives.

With our work so greatly amplified and broadcast by technology, it's incumbent upon us to do it well.

Some useful perspectives

This mini library of books is about e-learning. There's actually much confusion about what e-learning is and how beneficial it is beyond its cost savings.

The first confusion isn't much easier to resolve than the second, and both are frustratingly difficult to address concisely.

Definition 1. *The term e-learning applies to the broad range of ways computing and communication technologies can be used for teaching and learning. Some uses are effective—magnificently so. Others are not.*

This definition might get a passing grade on an exam and is similar to frequently cited definitions, but it nevertheless misses the essence of the thing. It's like defining an American football game

e-Learning

Drills
Instructional Games
Tutorials
Self-assessments
Bulletins
Webcasts
Reference Documents
EPSS
Problem-solving exercises
Simulations
LMS
Virtual Classrooms

as players trying to get the ball past the opposing team. It's like defining haute cuisine as good food, or great music as playing notes at the right times. Not wrong, but not sufficient either.

Perhaps the biggest problem is that this definition is so inclusive. Although it is true that one can learn from almost anything—a rubber band, toy assembly instructions, a seesaw, an episode of "The Simpsons"—we wouldn't generally call these learning materials. It is similarly inappropriate when people think electronically distributed presentations constitute e-learning, when no learning context is provided. Simply converting marketing brochures to .pdf files and distributing them to employees, for example, is not e-learning. In other words, e-publishing is not e-learning, and it's detrimental when they are confused with each other.

Definition 2. *e-Learning is delivery of carefully constructed instructional events through computing technologies.* It seems unfortunately necessary, because this form of instructional delivery is not inherently superior or inferior to other forms of delivery, to again add qualification: *Some e-learning events are effective—magnificently so. Others are not.*

This definition of e-learning is more useful because it excludes simple communication by computer and electronic distribution of documents (e-publishing or e-casting), unless they are used in a context configured for learning. Indeed, part of today's e-learning imbroglio, where today's high-impact learning activities are lumped together under the same heading with devastatingly boring and ineffective page-turners, is that we fail to use differentiating terms.

The figure above provides some clarity and differentiation to the concepts. It also recognizes that there are applications that bridge between them. Note that only some exemplary application types are included; new tools and forms of

e-Learning — Tutorials, Drills, Instructional Games, Problem-solving exercises, Simulations
e-Publishing — Bulletins, Reference Documents
Webcasts, Virtual Classrooms, EPSS, Self-assessments, LMS
Learning Tools

e-learning and e-publishing appear frequently.

As you form your own conception of e-learning, please note the following:

> The general approaches we can name now, such as simulation, tutorial, discovery, or problem solving, are merely examples of e-learning. They don't really define it.

> Minor variances make a huge difference. Change a little something, and you may have created an original design, and yet something that experts would readily include (or exclude from) within the rubric of e-learning.

> Some elaborate and expensive approaches achieve little learning or performance improvement; some simple and inexpensive ones have great impact.

e-Learning Babble

Many different types of learning events can be constructed, and because the varieties are truly infinite, they're difficult to name in useful ways. We can't come up with enough unique names for all of them. This means, unfortunately, that we don't have a very good vocabulary for comparative discussions of e-learning approaches, but indiscriminate use of the terms we do have makes matters worse.

Because there are so many different types of e-learning applications, even within our more narrowly focused definition, people and organizations considering e-learning for the first time often think too narrowly about it. You might yourself be thinking e-learning is the one type of application you have seen or imagined it to be without realizing the very broad array of possibilities.

The general definition, "delivery of carefully constructed instructional events through computing technologies," is good enough for those with casual interest and newspaper reporters, but who knows what kind of picture it paints for people who are truly curious and have never actually seen or understood e-learning? For them we need to be more specific, while remembering that there are surely additional forms of e-learning yet to be invented. We should also be open-minded enough, and even hopeful enough, to be thinking future forms of e-learning may cause

Think | What are three ways the Internet could be used to create otherwise impractical learning experiences?

us to expand, if not significantly restructure, the core concept as we see it today.

Resources

💻 A collection of definitions can be found at: www.e-learningconsulting. com/consulting/what/otherdefinitions. html

💻 And more at: www.google.com/ search?q=define:e-learning

Classes of e-learning

Applications of e-learning can be divided into two classes, synchronous and asynchronous. *Synchronous* learning events occur simultaneously for all learners as happens in classrooms when an instructor delivers a lecture. Examples of synchronous e-learning include instructional uses of web conferencing, live chat rooms, instant messaging, and virtual classrooms.

Asynchronous learning events are learning events that happen at different times for each learner, ideally when and as needed by each. Asynchronous e-learning includes self-paced courses, historically the most common form of e-learning, as well as message boards, discussion

forums, and mentoring through email.

Self-paced applications are frequently delivered to individual learners over a network, although physical duplication and distribution, such as on CD-ROMs, is still used. When the communications and individualizing capabilities of the Web or Internet are utilized, instead of simply its broadcasting capabilities, they can enhance learning experiences in important ways and provide unique learning opportunities.

Math problems, for example, can be based on today's price of oil. Learners can race each other, even forming teams matched on measures of competency, and check a live scoreboard.

Applications using the Internet for any purpose are, unfortunately, all lumped together and currently called *Web-Based Training* (WBT). When both synchronous and asynchronous approaches are used, we have a third category called *blended* learning.

Although there's a tendency to define different forms of e-learning by the enabling technologies they use, it's much more helpful if we focus on the different goals each category of e-learning is designed to

synchronous

asynchronous

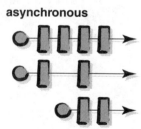

achieve, the different ways they go about it, the attributes that make them more or less appropriate for specific uses, and the successes they produce.

e-Learning isn't about learning

Ok, it is about learning. But you almost shouldn't think of it that way. *Learning* is a term that's unfortunately associated for many people with having to sit still for too long. It conjures up the anxiety of being called on to answer questions of apparent interest to a teacher, but not necessarily to you. It's associated with sacrificing active times for book time, cramming for tests, getting grades.

We need not only fresh ways of thinking about learning, but also fresh ways of making it happen. Why? Learning is really about performance improvement (and happiness, I might add). It's about preparing for life's opportunities and challenges. It's about making changes that are necessary for competency and fulfillment. Learning is essential to success, both individual and organizational. If you keep doing things the same old way, how can you expect anything to improve?

e-Learning is about success

e-Learning is really about enabling new, more effective behaviors. It's about providing ever more beneficial ways of helping individuals and organizations acquire new skills and access knowledge.

Can it work? Without question. In this book and others, you'll find examples and references to e-learning applications that have not only reduced training costs, but have increased both individual and organizational performance astoundingly.

Does it work? Only when it's designed and built properly. And that's what this book is here to help you do.

The secrets are out

Based on the best practices of the studios at Allen Interactions and literally decades of work in the production of learning experiences, this book shares openly and freely with you the many lessons learned about developing successful e-learning.

There is much more to it, of course, than you can read in a book. But what's not included in this series is best learned on the job. Go to it and spread success!

Feb. 28, 2006 Michael W. Allen

Part One
Organizational Realities

Easy as pie. Wilma Allen made heavenly pies. She was my mother, so you might think I'm biased in this judgment. But I'm not. Everyone who ever took one bite of her pies sighed that unmistakable sigh of delight that comes from tasting the best ever.

During one of my years in graduate school, the Ohio State Fair started a "Teach Someone to Make a Pie" contest. We thought it would be fun.

Under her watchful eye, I'd measure things according to the recipe. Easy enough, but then she'd say, "Put in a little more." *Why?* "It doesn't look like enough. I usually put in more." *But the recipe... Ok.*

"How warm are your hands?" Huh? "Let me feel them. Oh, warm. Mine are always cold. That will make a difference." *Huh?*

We laughed and struggled. I never once got a crust transferred to the pie pan in one piece. "We could reduce the shortening and that will make it much easier for you. Of course, the crust will be tough and not as flakey." *Hmm, do we have to?* "I don't know. I'm not having that problem. See." Hers rolled out and transferred perfectly.

Mom later admitted she had never had success teaching anyone to make pies like hers. She decided she'd never try teaching pie making again, and I realized I'd never learn. Those incredible pies are just a precious memory now.

What's the value of transmitting your best practices?

There are many challenges to meet in transmitting best practices from one individual to another. They are compounded when attempting to develop a program to transmit them to multiple people. Add in the complexities of physical separation, such as a national or worldwide workforce, perhaps students from different cultures, or frequently changing content, and you have a big challenge indeed.

e-Learning provides delivery cost and convenience advantages as well as the ability to adapt to individual learner needs and provide personalized practice. As a standalone solution or blended with other forms of instruction, e-learning offers great potential, but as with all forms of instruction, e-learning is effective only when it is focused on real needs and designed well to meet them.

Unfortunately, much of today's e-learning is not designed well. And much of it is not focused on individual or organizational needs so that it makes much of a difference to anyone. Among the many factors that contribute to this disappointing state are crippling misconceptions— misconceptions about learning itself, misconceptions about the capabilities of e-learning, misconceptions about who needs to be involved in the process of learning application development.

Part One of this book focuses briefly on several typical scenarios we'll follow throughout the book. They reveal the ways sensible people make ineffective choices about e-learning and prevent it from being the valued resource it has the ready potential to be.

Chapter 1 – The Corporate Skeptic

An executive wants to reduce training costs and increase sales. He is skeptical of e-learning even though he is quite unfamiliar with it. He'd like some proof of effectiveness before taking a risk, as this would be his organization's first foray into e-learning.

Chapter 2 – Academic Woes

The new director of training at a university hospital is charged with converting parts of their curriculum created and currently taught by their faculty into e-learning. An instructional designer by both education and previous experience, she will be leading the in-house team to "repurpose" their materials using the ADDIE process.

Chapter 3 – Hesitant Explorers

A pharmaceutical company has been unsuccessful with off-the-shelf e-learning. After abandoning e-learning for a while, they are now entertaining the thought that custom-designed applications might fare better.

Chapter 4 – Grasping the Whole Challenge

There are many challenges to confront in designing and building powerful e-learning, but the biggest problems usually have nothing to do with technology or instructional design. They emanate from organizational behaviors, such as the tendency of decision-makers to refrain from personal involvement at critical times.

In This Part

1 | The Corporate Skeptic

Jim Sanders doesn't have a lot of interest in training, let alone e-learning. As VP of Sales at Step Up Ladders, Inc., Jim is well-known for his ready quip, "Best training I ever had was being thrown in the lake. Learned to swim mighty fast. No videotapes, whiteboards, or any fancy stuff."

He's thinking more seriously about alternatives than he lets on. He's being careful because he could expose the fact that his opinions reflect more of a doubt that anyone can learn much from a computer than any evidence he has against it. On the other hand, no one has brought him evidence that proves a great return on investment for e-learning. He feels right to be skeptical.

But Jim really can't afford to overlook a way to cut his training costs. So he's reluctantly, and quite privately, thinking he needs to size up e-learning, whatever it is.

Яapid reader

- There are good reasons to be skeptical of e-learning.

- Not all e-learning has equivalent value.

- e-Learning isn't about learning; it's about performance improvement and success.

Show and tell

Step Up Ladders is the first of three contextual scenarios I'll use to present the challenges e-learning has in meeting the needs of today's organizations. Designers and developers of high-impact e-learning meet plenty of challenge just in creating effective learning events. But their work isn't nearly that simple. They must also guide decision-makers who are often not ready to use e-learning to greatest advantage. Knowing only that many organizations are claiming great advantages, they may not even have a very clear picture of what e-learning is.

e-Learning is hard to describe and harder yet to define, because it takes many forms. It's like the proverbial elephant—until you've seen one, or at least a picture of one, verbal descriptions may leave you feeling knowledgeable when you're still quite uninformed.

Defining e-learning seems to be even more challenging than defining an elephant. Unless you intend to care for elephants or will encounter them in the wild, simply seeing any elephant probably imparts enough working information. But seeing even several exemplary e-learning applications doesn't impart enough to make you either an informed connoisseur or a proficient designer. It is, however, an invaluable start.

Core components

Anyone considering e-learning, whether as a buyer, user, or developer, should begin by looking at some examples. Look for its four core components:

> ➤ Multimedia
> ➤ Interactivity
> ➤ Computation
> ➤ Communication

Multimedia capabilities present information or "content" graphically and textually. Sounds, animation, and video are also available to provide rich attention-getting presentations that can help learners grasp concepts quickly and more fully.

Interactivity provides the means for asking questions, selecting challenges, and presenting feedback to learners. Learners generally give their responses through use of a computer mouse and keyboard, although some systems recognize spoken responses, display screen touch, and other gestures.

Perhaps most importantly and frequently underused, e-learning systems offer rapid *computation*. Instructional logic and electronically updated performance records can determine the sequence of events to individualize the experience and adapt it to each learner's abilities and goals. Computational logic can generate exercises that match each learner's needs to make steady, personalized progress toward proficiency. Computation can provide simulations that make learning contexts more realistic and help transfer training to real-world performance.

A fourth component, *communication* with databases and other users, is possible through network connection. When these facilities are used, as in the synchronous and asynchronous forms of e-learning mentioned above, learner communities can be formed to motivate individuals, enrich the experience, and provide a broad complement of both structured learning events and informal learning opportunities.

Communication capabilities enable Learning Management Systems (LMS) to register learners, specify learning paths, and record progress. An LMS makes practical the provision of e-learning activities to large numbers of people and further facilitates interweaving other learning experiences into blended learning solutions.

As with so many things, listing the components of e-learning doesn't provide a very comprehensible picture. It's how all the pieces are fitted together in each application that creates an e-learning application, an e-publishing application, or something else.

Because e-learning can provide experiences that optimize each learner's time, adapt sequencing to address specific goals and competencies, and provide the practice needed to perform confidently on the job and in life, e-learning clearly has valuable attributes beyond it's lower cost delivery, around-the-clock availability, and consistency. But, of course, it does have these attractive attributes as well.

Prove it

"I hear the pluses. Some of this does make sense, but show me data. Prove to me that e-learning works," demands *Jim.*

Jim is being reasonable, maybe even open-minded. The demand for justification doesn't indicate negative prejudgment, even though it sometimes irritates proponents of e-learning. But he is asking a question that's much more complicated than it looks to him, and perhaps to anyone at first.

There is evidence. Many of today's better books on e-learning list studies that demonstrate successful outcomes. For example, Nick van Dam's book presents twenty-five case studies that achieved major business goals. (See list on p. 8.)

These studies prove, without doubt, that e-learning can work and does work—sometimes, at least. They do not prove that e-learning always works. And, of course (I can't believe I'm writing this), it depends on what your definition of "works" is.

"Obviously, to attract senior executive support and to contribute real value to the organization, the main objective of e-learning must be to create or enhance the shareholder value—the company's growth in profitability and value in the marketplace—by linking e-learning initiative to the business drivers and by proposing a value proposition for future investments in e-learning." (van Dam, 2004, p. 9)

van Dam Case Studies of Business Goals Achieved Through e-Learning

The e-Learning Fieldbook: Implementation Lessons and Case Studies from Companies That Are Making e-Learning Work. Nick van Dam. (2004, p. 9). New York: McGraw-Hill.

- ➤ Expeditious time-to-market of new products and services
- ➤ Rapid implementation of new information systems and business process
- ➤ Complete compliance with legal and regulatory mandates
- ➤ Efficient on-boarding of new hires in the organization
- ➤ Integration of a global workforce and creation of a strong business culture
- ➤ Enhanced leadership and generation of new business development
- ➤ Improved sales by developing a knowledgeable and effective sales force
- ➤ Effective retention of customers and suppliers through training in products and services

The complication in Jim's simple request for proof comes from the fact that every implementation of a training solution, including e-learning solutions, is different. The learners, their motivations and capabilities, the environment and expectations, the history and reputation of training within the organization, the consequences of poor and outstanding performance, the content complexity, and many other factors combine to make situations different.

Let me ask you a question. Are movies entertaining?

Probably no one ever asked you this because it's a silly question. If someone did ask you, you'd reply that not all movies are alike. Some are entertaining, some are educational, some are painful, and some are boring.

Now consider this question. Does training work? If you asked this question, almost everyone would answer, "Yes. Well, sometimes." They'd typically hasten to qualify it, "It depends on how good it is, of course." Of course. Not all e-learning is effective, but since some of it is, it's clear that the technology has the capability to deliver powerful learning experiences.

You can certainly "prove" to Jim that e-learning works sometimes, and hasten to qualify your position that not all e-learning is alike, just as all books and all movies are not alike. (Can you imagine anyone making the demand, "Prove to me that books work?" They do—sometimes. Why not always? You answer.)

Success with e-learning

We can list the components of a book and even the components of a great story, but that doesn't tell us how to write a great book nor even what exactly constitutes a great book. You have to experience a great book (or movie or park or ball game), and maybe a few poor ones too, before you can recognize the good ones and know what's possible.

It seems unlikely anyone is going to write a great book without ever having read one, but it seems even more unlikely that anyone is going to create great e-learning on a budget and schedule without having experienced any. And success seems very remote indeed if the process is catch as catch can.

I think I can help. After literally decades of developing e-learning applications, together with teaching and mentoring others as well, it's clear that many people employ mental models, design ideals, and

processes that are not helpful. They target the wrong behaviors (often being misled unwittingly and unintentionally by their clients), build to the wrong design criteria, and use a process that pretty much ignores these disastrous risks.

Seemingly small differences, even differences undetectable at first, can make a huge difference in outcomes. In truth, every e-learning design project is a combination of applied principles and experimentation. (See Driscoll & Carliner, 2005.) One shouldn't be discouraged, however, because the results are often spectacular. There are two big points here: (1) not all e-learning has equivalent value to an organization and (2) in order to maximize chances that an application will achieve great value, it's critical to use an effective process for design and development. I'm talking about a process that efficiently gets issues on the table, cuts through confounded assumptions and organizational entanglements, explores alternatives, sets appropriate criteria, and uses time and resources productively.

A process that meets these criteria is *successive approximation*. And that's what this book is about.

2 | Academic Woes

Robin Taylor is excited about the enthusiastic support and the $50,000 budget she has at Wakefield Medical University to convert their training into e-learning. As the director of training, Robin was originally hired to take the hospital into the e-learning era and now, after much discussion of budget, content, schedule, and logistics, she's actually getting the green light for their first project.

Robin was an instructional designer for her previous employer and had the opportunity to work on a couple of e-learning projects that won nods of approval. Although she isn't expecting it to be easy, Robin is sure she can lead this ready, able, and willing team to great success with e-learning.

The university instructors created the current curriculum that they also teach. Robin admires the skills of the staff and figures that with all the existing curricular materials and experience teaching, they have great prospects for success by reformatting their content for e-learning presentation.

It's quiet in the eye of the storm

But mosey out just a bit, as Robin is about to do, and it's anything but soft summer breezes. Right?

Robin has in-house curriculum developers who are expert in the subjects to be taught. They also have extensive teaching experience and familiarity with the learner audience.

The existing curriculum was prepared for classroom delivery. It includes lesson plans, bullet-point slides, and display graphics. Presentation material is cross-referenced to a basic text, and additional reading resources (reprints, white papers, etc.) are also on hand. Tests have been developed, complete with answer keys and grading standards.

On top of all this, the administration is already sold on e-learning and anticipates great success with it. Economically, the organization has justified development of proprietary e-learning courses based simply on the reduction of train-

**Primary Phases of the
ADDIE Proccess**

ing costs. If the training becomes more effective, as some think it will be, there will be additional benefits.

It is easy to see why Robin is excited about her new position. In her previous work, she's seen how to get an e-learning project completed and rolled out. She's learned the basics: begin with Analysis, then undertake Design, Development, Implementation, and finish up with Evaluation (ADDIE). It's easy to remember and understand ADDIE. It's a process that's been used for decades.

We'll talk more about ADDIE a bit later.

Where's the problem?

Here's a list of eleven potential problems. Check off those you think are likely problems for Robin at University Hospital.

- ❑ Conflicting expectations
- ❑ Instructor-led training as a model for e-learning
- ❑ Insufficient content
- ❑ Focus on content

- ❑ Plan to repurpose materials
- ❑ Project management expertise
- ❑ Technical expertise
- ❑ ADDIE process
- ❑ Justification based on cost-reduction
- ❑ Cost of the project
- ❑ Need for a blended learning solution

Did you find a likely problem? Or several? More? Try it this way: cross out the ones you can eliminate.

Doing it all wrong

Robin wasn't quite sure how to divide up her budget, but she needed some plan to start with. She made up a table that seemed to reflect a reasonable distribution. (see budget on next page).

Thinking she had about $7,500 to complete an analysis, Robin enthusiastically consulted the most experienced instructors to determine how to proceed most efficiently. Marilyn Stoffer had been with the university for nearly fifteen years

Robin's e-Learning Budget

	Percent	Cost
Analysis	15	$7,500
Design	25	$12,500
Development	35	$17,500
Implementation	20	$10,000
Evaluation	5	$2,500
	100	$50,000

and, with an endearing smile, let Robin know how wise she was to come to her first.

"Robin, we've been at this for a long time," Marilyn said, "and, frankly, the administration doesn't know what they'd be throwing away if we jumped willy-nilly into e-learning thinking computers can do what our staff is doing every day here. I know we have cost pressures and a need to increase enrollment. But I say we'd best use what money we have to hire more instructors.

"I'm afraid this isn't what the administration wants to hear, and I know I'm not going to change their minds. I really don't want to be on the wrong side of things either, so let me suggest this. Let's

just focus in on some of the basic stuff everyone needs to know, like terms and definitions, job roles and responsibilities, and so on. It will be a useful piece to show and use. Just leave the real teaching to us."

Robin appreciated Marilyn's attempt to be constructive and recognized for the first time the fear her instructors had that e-learning might cause job loss. She also began to recognize that instructors had a vested interest in relegating mundane content to e-learning, possibly causing it to fail—an outcome the instructors might secretly applaud.

Getting the support of the staff was going to be difficult, let alone achieving an enthusiastic buy-in. And then there was the staff's inex-

Can you list more potential problems?

Think

perience in designing e-learning. Could she teach them the necessary skills and concepts as part of the project?

More problems?

Are there even more potential problems?

Before you read on, think about the context and expectations. Are there more potential, even likely, problems?

> How about learner access to computers (she may have made some bad assumptions here) and IT support (if it's absent, yikes!)?

> How comfortable are students with using computers? Will students see e-learning as beneficial or yet another depersonalized cost-savings program? Are student advisors involved and supportive?

> Is $50,000 a reasonable budget? It sounds like a lot of money. To Robin, it feels like her abilities have been recognized through the trust that comes from having a $50,000 budget. She knows she'll be able to do something for this amount, and if it doesn't go far enough, she'll ask for more when the time is right. Good plan?

> What's the expected schedule? Will instructors be given lighter training loads so they'll have time to work on e-learning? When will they be available and for how long? Is this sufficient? How could Robin or anyone possibly know at this point?

Better check each one of the potential problems listed previously, cross out none, and make room for more.

Armed and ready

There are many reasons e-learning projects never achieve the impact they could have. Developers are often disappointed that so many compromises were made along the way. No matter how able any one or group is to design powerfully engaging e-learning, projects are often crippled by underestimating the challenge.

As you contemplate any e-learning development project, it's important to prepare for the complexity of the undertaking. Using a tried-and-true process will arm you well for both the expected and unexpected challenges, and bolster your confidence. And help you maintain your enthusiastic commitment to excellence.

3 | Hesitant Explorers

Zanick Pharmaceuticals has had award-winning training practices almost since the founding of the company in 1946. Founders Brett and Bartholomew Zanick believed, long before it became a popular precept, that knowledge is power that should be aggressively distributed throughout an organization.

Zanick values face-to-face contact and personal mentoring. It steered clear of e-learning for a long time, thinking it was mostly a solution in search of a problem. But with training costs becoming a major issue, and the variety and frequency of training needs continuing to increase, Zanick took a look at e-learning by licensing some off-the-shelf products.

This was a disaster. Students hated the impersonal nature of the training and failed to complete lessons. Supervisors reported increasing requests for help and decreased worker knowledge.

Although training costs did drop a bit, everyone felt e-learning was the wrong path. Even management became concerned after a while.

In desperate need for consistent and brilliantly effective training that was both easy to update and easy to disseminate worldwide, Zanick revisited e-learning. As an experiment, Emily Hayes, CLO, directed George Sharpe, Director of Security Training, to build some custom e-learning. This e-learning would reflect Zanick's expectations and values. Its goal as a pilot project: determine the potential value of e-learning as a method of training Zanick employees.

Where do you start?

George and Emily had long discussions about where to start. They began by listing some of the things they knew would be important:

➤ The skills to be learned
➤ Current learner abilities
➤ Multimedia capabilities supported by the in-house network
➤ The activities learners would benefit from
➤ Activities that would appeal to Zanick employees

➢ Behavioral objectives

➢ Content to be covered

➢ Currently available content

➢ Technical standards and requirements

➢ Current performance errors prioritized by cost

➢ Attributes desired in e-learning

➢ Budget and schedule

➢ Needed and available subject-matter experts

➢ Identifying who is in charge of what and who should be involved with what

As the list grew longer and longer, they found themselves thinking this project would never get off the ground. The funding for covering all these issues would more than consume the entire amount they expected to spend for the development of their training. And this activity was all a precursor to development. It wouldn't include any development at all!

Each listed item is important, and carefully scrutinizing them all would be a valuable activity. But a thorough analysis of all these items cannot be done quickly. Most items will consume many hours of data gathering, analysis, and consensus building.

George went to the company's centralized training development group. They had a few people experienced in e-learning design and development, although they were currently assigned to different work. He asked for some of their time and showed them his list.

"Where do you start?" he asked. "I mean, all this seems really important."

"Yes," they agreed, "these are critical items, for sure. And there are more. You'd better get with IT, for example, as soon as possible and let them know what you want to do. They're sticklers about what they will and won't allow to run on our systems.

"If you want to use any video, for example, they'll really be concerned about bandwidth. They'll want to know whose computers you plan to use, what software you're going to run, how it will link with the HR system, and more things than I can name. They're particularly interested in who is going to support all this, of course."

This was bad news for George. Instead of helping, they were only making the challenge seem insurmountable. If he talked with IT, how could he answer their inevi-

table questions? He would need IT's support, of course, but he truly didn't know yet what his technology requirements were going to be.

George thought he should test the water and had a brief conversation with IT Director Marty Markson. Marty explained that there really were a lot of issues involved. They ran into many unexpected issues with the commercial training packages they had tried, and he, for one, was glad Zanick had backed off. On the other hand, Marty said their systems were much more powerful now and e-learning didn't seem to have requirements very different from those of email; then again, email support was demanding a sizable budget.

Marty suggested that George contract with an outside consulting firm to come in to analyze their situation and prepare a report for him and upper management to review.

Making simple things simple again

It's pretty amazing how organizations can make the use of technology for learning so complicated. It's true that the blend of instruction and technology is multidimensional. It gets into drama and theatrics, learning theory, graphic design, perception, creative writing, technical writing, game and simulation design, data management, communications, and more. But a lot of things that we do successfully and with some ease appear dauntingly complicated when we itemize all their components.

Getting started down the right track with e-learning requires assessing the situation, identifying the key players and getting their involvement, setting reasonable goals, and using an effective process. When beginners start out in e-learning, they often make the mistake of trying too hard to do everything perfectly. They end up moving too slowly, missing the big opportunities, and—if they don't simply give up along the way—producing something boring and awful, much to their chagrin. These are all fatal errors that can be prevented.

> **Think**
>
> Begin listing in your head all the steps you would take to drive to Home Depot and return home with a purchase of 200 grit sandpaper. Does the list of decisions and actions make it seem like a truly impossible task?

4 | Grasping the Whole Challenge

Organizations are as unique as their constituents. Although they may face similar challenges as other organizations, their individual experience, personalities, and problem-solving styles determine what works and what doesn't work for them. Individuals determine whether smart mistakes are seen as progress or intolerable performance. They determine whether simply following the rules is success or whether achieving targeted outcomes is.

Developing a successful training program is a complex challenge. It's made far more complex, unfortunately, because it must typically be created in a context of many diverse interests and address a number of personal and bureaucratic goals as well. Any process that ignores the total context, its subtleties and its effects, is unlikely to succeed.

ᴙapid reader

- A successful process focuses not only on instructional design and development, but also on helping the organization define its greatest needs and opportunities.

- Seven typical, but bad, assumptions about instructional product development are listed.

- It's critical to get both the support and participation of the right people, not just their delegates.

Real-world contexts

Jim Sanders, VP of Sales at Step Up Ladders, feels uncertain. As a leader, it's painful to him when he lacks confidence in his decision-making readiness. He's heard the many claims for what e-learning can do, but they have the ring of hyperbole. He isn't a trainer and probably hasn't experienced a lot of training to which he would accredit his personal success. But if e-learning could meet his needs and cut costs, he'd feel accountable for bypassing an important opportunity. He's not afraid of risks, but he is afraid of wasting valuable time and resources. What's he to do?

Working at a university hospital, Robin Taylor has highly motivated, rushed and impatient learners. There is complex legal regulation and high performance liability. As a project manager and former instructional designer, she's energized by her organization's trust the $50,000 project budget conveys and is eager to lead her in-house team of instructors in converting instructor-led training to e-learning. Almost instantly, however, she discovered that she's in a crossfire between *the administration's goals and the instructors'. How does she solve this problem and also develop a quality training solution that stands up to stringent scrutiny?*

Zanick Pharmaceuticals directed George Sharpe to prove that e-learning can work for them. He's never developed e-learning before and knows from experience with some bad off-the-shelf courseware that e-learning isn't always a good thing. Employees didn't like it, and the desired outcome performance levels weren't achieved. The CLO has her eyes on him, and his failure could mean the loss of his job—and maybe even hers. Should he risk admitting he doesn't know how to develop their first project internally and bring in an outside vendor, or should he just give it his best try?

It takes a village…

Jim needs to fess up about his concerns, overcome his disabling notion that training isn't his job, and get the real scoop on e-learning and also learn the strengths and weaknesses of other skill-building approaches. He isn't going to get statistical proof that an as-yet-to-be-developed e-learning program will achieve everything he needs. He's even going to find

it hard to get a firm price on what a satisfactory e-learning solution will cost, unless he gets involved. Delegation isolates him from the information he needs to make good decisions. He knows that, but he isn't really fond of training. Trainers never seem as interested in business challenges as they are in their theories, techniques, and whatever else it is they do.

It isn't going to work for Robin or George to go off on their own either, although this is what many training development groups do. Get the funding, disappear, try like heck to meet the schedule and budget. Even if their work received an A rating from e-learning experts, it would be unlikely to meet the organization's highest priority needs or to receive the necessary support. Regardless of your design and project management expertise, you're liable to miss the biggest opportunity by a significant margin if you're deprived of the involvement of those who own the performance challenges, are responsible for achieving goals, and benefit from success.

It takes the involvement and live-in participation of a village to succeed with e-learning. The two-camp approach doesn't work with management living in one camp, training in another. It would be something like one group being out in front, strategically commanding a battle, while another group was guessing what strategies the command was going to take and being responsible for having the appropriate resources developed and placed as needed. Certain disaster.

Much of the attention devoted to the process of e-learning design and development over the last half-century has focused on organizing content and developing learning programs efficiently. While many of us find inadequacies in typical processes used to develop desired learning experiences, these processes are prone to even worse faults. They tend to exclude and even ignore the camp in command.

Dangerous assumptions

Three dangerous assumptions have led to many failures:

1. WRONG: Managers know what they want and what their people need.

It is, indeed, management's job to know these things, but without recognizing the full range of training possibilities—especially recent technology-enhanced possibilities— managers tend to set anemic, ineffective goals for training.

"Make sure all our clerks know the return policy." Regardless of what is said, management doesn't really care whether clerks know the policy or not. What's important is that the policy be executed properly, courteously, and consistently. This is a different goal, and not a goal that will be achieved simply through having everyone memorize policy.

2. WRONG: Management shouldn't be involved in instructional design.

It's a pretty new thought for both managers and instructional designers that management should be involved in designing training solutions. In fact, most designers work to keep the agnostics out of the consecrated process of learning design.

"They'll just push their personal preferences and agenda, which are often at odds with or just simply irrelevant to what makes a good instructional program." Use of jargon and references to learning theory helps make outsiders uncomfortable and protects the instructional designer's turf.

Unfortunately, it's in the early design activity where many options can be seen and evaluated for the first time. It's an important opportunity to reevaluate the goal and its alignment to top organizational priorities. It's when budgetary and other constraints can be evaluated most effectively and alternatives considered. This is where and when management can and needs to play a vital role.

3. WRONG: It takes extensive and costly research to sufficiently analyze needs to propose appropriate solutions.

Indeed, there's no limit on how much time and effort can be put into up-front analysis. But it's not smart to tarry here, regardless of available capital. The reasons to do this as fast as possible and move on are plentiful. Consider this one. Dynamic organizations have rapidly changing needs. If you have spent a long time analyzing needs, the needs you analyzed and so meticulously documented may no longer be the current or the highest priority needs. You can miss the critical window for developing and delivering training if you're paralyzed by analysis. Quicker, less extensive (and less

costly) research can prove to be much more valuable.

Not just any village will do

We need certain participants to speak up at the right times. There's a tendency, whether just to make scheduling meetings easier or to move things along faster, to exclude input from those people who are actually in the best position to provide direction, make binding decisions, and improve the prospects of a successful project.

It's important to get the invitation list right, and not to prejudge the contributions that can be made from different perspectives. By limiting the information you have, you might make progress simpler at first, but there's increased likelihood that you're missing something important. Whether it's going off in the wrong direction or finding later on that you don't have the good will and positive support you need, what appears to be simplification here could be stacking the cards against your success.

More dangerous assumptions

Yes, we have more typical, dangerous assumptions. These assumptions also frequently lead to the wrong list of participants.

4. WRONG: As instructional designers, we know what learners like and appreciate.

"I'm a person," thinks the designer. "And I was a student for many years too. I know what people like and don't like."

Learners behave differently, use different standards, and value things differently in the various situations in which they find themselves. As we've previously noted, learning and performance contexts strongly influence our perceptions and our behaviors.

Is this mandated training? We expect not to like most things that are mandated. After all, if it were so helpful and pleasant, would it have to be mandated? We often find ourselves looking for faults in anything mandated, almost as an automatic response.

Does it get me a certificate and a higher salary? Does it make my life easier? If I'm not getting anything out this that I want, I'm probably not going to be fully engaged.

Is it using up valuable time and putting me further behind?

Understanding the learner

perspective is critical to success in changing behavior. So is realizing that learners differ from each other. They represent a range of perspectives as well as a range of abilities. You can't teach people things they already know; you can only frustrate them in the attempt.

Good designers don't make assumptions here. They don't circumvent learners. They involve them. There's really no other way to a great success.

5. WRONG: Subject-matter experts know what learners will understand.

Being expert in the subject to be learned almost guarantees you will not be able to see things through the eyes and mind of a learner. SMEs are great for validating what we are teaching, and even though they may currently be teaching, I often find a surprising disconnect between what learners find clear and helpful and what SMEs think is helpful instruction.

There's no need to make assumptions here, we should verify everything with the true experts on what learners will understand: the learners.

6. WRONG: Subject-matter experts know what learners need to learn.

It may sound like I'm blaming subject-matter experts for the causes and misfortunes of poor e-learning design. I'm not. No, the problem lies in how we use these valuable human resources.

SMEs can be expected to provide thorough content that is true and accurate. They should be able to identify best practices, performance standards, and typical errors and their causes.

But there is no obligation for training to include all this material nor to organize it in any way similar to the organization that makes best sense to SMEs. In fact, it's highly unlikely that the SME's organization of content will be optimal sequencing for learners.

More importantly, subject-matter experts are not usually expert in the analysis of the behavioral faults of learners. Although they may be able to construct good posttests, SMEs are not typically in a position to know what learners know, what they need to learn, nor what prevents them from performing optimally. Rather, it is those people who supervise performance who are in the optimal position to know and relate to all the details of real-world performance. And, of course, to the performers themselves.

7. WRONG: Learners can't be helpful until we've developed the instruction.

I've already asserted that learners are, indeed, the true experts on what can help them. Their actual responses to designs, not necessarily their verbalized requests and predictions of what would be good, tell us whether the design is successful or not. But we certainly don't want to wait until we've completed the project, exhausted the budget, and run out of time to make changes before we get this feedback.

The solution here is to draw on a mixture of learners—some who have yet to learn the subject and others who have recently learned it. Recent learners can remember not knowing the content and not being able to perform the targeted skills. They can tell us what helped them learn—the meaningful steppingstones and the aha moments.

Learners who have not yet tackled the subject can acquaint us with the typical entry skills, motivations, and computer interface contrivances they can handle. We can test ideas by having them work through prototypes, describe their interest in getting some training, and tell us what they like and don't like about being a part of their organizations. Responses at this point are almost always surprising and extraordinarily helpful for training design.

A clear vision

Ok, what does a review of these dangerous, yet common assumptions tell us? It tells us that getting to the essence of the organization is important, just as is understanding learners and the environment in which they'll work. We need input and actual agreement from a cross section of the organization, which means a group of people who would rarely, if ever, congregate.

Who's coming to dinner?

Probably not the typical collection of guests, but having the right participants will very much determine how successful the event is. Although our guests might be a bit uneasy at first in the mixed group we've invited, they'll come to appreciate getting to know each other's views as they've probably never known them before. They'll quickly realize how valuable

this small assembly is and want to do more projects together.

Let's quickly review who needs to participate in the process and why.

Budget makers can't allocate effectively for training projects when they really have no idea of what can and should be accomplished—and without adequate funding, what can't and won't be accomplished. They need to be there, in person, to learn and guide.

Our party needs to include the *person who owns the performance problem*, as this is often, and unfortunately, not the budget maker. We're also hoping to have a *person who supervises the performance* of people we're teaching. In a university, college, or school, we must generally entrust the teacher or professor to reflect both of these viewpoints.

Our event also needs to include *someone who knows the content thoroughly* to be sure we impart best practices and valid information. Our guest list needs to include *candidate learners* to help make sure that what we are doing is appealing, interesting, understandable, and usable to them. *Recent learners* would be most welcome to give us insights about what helped them learn this specific content and what was a hindrance. In some instances, recent learners are more helpful than almost anyone else.

Finally, the organization's *project leader* needs to be present, as this person will be the point of contact for the e-learning team, helping to get information, schedule reviews, and do many tasks, most of which are time-sensitive. This person needs not only the responsibility but also the clout to make things happen.

Involvement of each of these representatives is truly critical. The discussion can't be just the training group talking among themselves.

Meeting the challenge

The obvious question is how to do all this efficiently. How can we educate non-educators about the possibilities and support needs of alternative solutions? How can we include divergent opinions, reach consensus, and win support for a solution everyone understands?

The answer is a process that recognizes the contextual complexity of solution development, the typical need for client education, and the need for invention as opposed to simple principle application. The answer is *Successive Approximation*.

Part Two

Escaping Tradition

But it's always done that way. Ever had the *pleasure* of building a new house or remodeling one? My wife and I have undertaken such projects on perhaps too many occasions, always thinking the process is going to run more smoothly than the last time. It probably would if we weren't always trying to get our builders to do something out of the ordinary.

Creativity is, by definition, doing something differently and possibly better. At the very least, it's a chance to accomplish something that's interesting.

On a flight not too long ago, I sat next to a fellow who heads a large residential construction firm. He saw me reading a copy of *Fine Homebuilding* magazine and asked if I were a carpenter. "Only as a hobby," I said. "We're rebuilding our house that was damaged by Hurricane Ivan."

"Looking for new ideas and products, I suppose," he said, with a noticeable trace of distain. "Sure," I replied. "I'm fascinated by new products. There's always something new to know about."

"No offense," he said, "but I wouldn't want you as a client. And I wish they'd stop putting out magazines like that one. They just get everybody excited about newfangled gadgets that we don't know how to install." *Newfangled!*

Want e-learning that's old and stodgy, static and boring, focused on content presentation instead of a powerful learning experience? The old methods work fine for that. Want something better and more interesting? You might look for a new design and development process.

Does your process focus on getting the content right or on making the learning experience memorable?

I have many times apologized publicly to my students who learned development processes from me that have produced boring and wasteful e-learning. It's not that these processes couldn't produce fun and energizing learning events; it's that they don't do so with any regularity. The problem is, in part, that they focused so much on doing things right, as opposed to doing the right things.

In this part of the book, I took a moment to look at what hasn't worked and why. There are lessons to be learned from the decades of e-learning development our field has now completed.

Change doesn't come easily, even when we want to improve. So I examine here what it takes to get started down a new path—one that uses a highly successful process called successive approximations. I am keeping no secrets and I am sharing with you, in detail, a process my studios and many successful development teams use to produce successful, award-winning e-learning applications.

Chapter 5 – Lessons from ADDIE

ADDIE stands for Analysis, Design, Development, Implementation, and Evaluation—a good list of the primary tasks to be performed in developing any learning program. Unfortunately, there have been so many diverging interpretations and adaptations of the ADDIE process that the name is no longer very descriptive and useful. Even worse, the most common applications of ADDIE are linear and tend to produce dreadful e-learning.

Chapter 6 – Making Useful Mistakes (ASAP)

The creative process is often one of trial and error. With today's technology, we don't have to take the energy-draining path, writing lengthy documents to describe what might be built and getting a round of approvals before we experiment with some design ideas. But to make experimental trial and error effective, it is important to set a goal and get the right team busy making useful mistakes.

Chapter 7 – Inalienable Risks

It's very easy to design learning programs. It's quite hard to design good ones. Unfortunately, the pitfalls often look like logical steps. One can confidently take the wrong path and not realize it until reaching its end. A good process strips pitfalls of their erudite guises and helps everyone, whether schooled in human learning or not, to succeed.

In This Part

5 | Lessons from ADDIE

Robin was glad she retained her design and development process materials from her previous job to share with her team at the hospital. She knew that speaking knowledgeably was important to bolster the team's confidence in her. After a little review, she made some presentation slides and was ready to go.

"First," she said at her kickoff meeting, "we'll start with analysis. And there's a lot to do. We need to analyze our current training methods for their strengths and weaknesses, determine whether we're training our students on exactly the right tasks, build our performance measures, then define our delivery program, and put together our budget."

Everyone rolled their eyes. And Robin felt her confidence slipping away after only one meeting. She expected this to be hard, but fun too. Creating new learning materials had been exciting work, but now she sensed what her whole team was barely holding back. There was going to be a ton of drudgery before they even started. And

worse, how much of her $50,000 budget would be spent before anything new was created?

Process virtuosity

Ever heard a group of beginners screeching through "Twinkle, Twinkle, Little Star" on the violin? Wincing from just your imagination? So am I, and we know the real experience is much worse.

I experience similar distress when I imagine Robin's team trying to produce their first e-learning. Remember, Robin is leading classroom instructors in an effort to repurpose the curricular materials they created for instructor-led delivery. She has a lead instructor who either doesn't know the capabilities of e-learning or doesn't see them and fears for her job, should e-learning succeed. Robin has never managed an e-learning design and development effort before, although she has e-learning design experience.

It takes practice to become adept at e-learning design and development. Beginners in e-learning (as in music) usually make a terrible racket at first. That's ok, unless your first effort will be used to determine the effectiveness of e-learning for the organization or other long-term decisions, such as your employment.

First efforts

e-Learning development is a skilled profession—actually, a combination of skilled professions, including instructional design, art and design, writing, programming, project management, and more. Everyone needs to work together in an organized, almost symphonic, fashion to do the job. Team members need to know what's expected of them and when they need to do their work. They need to understand the strengths and limitations of e-learning as well as critical principles of good instruction and the learning process.

Of course, every professional was a novice at one point, and everyone has his or her first projects to live through. A team like Robin's can learn and succeed, even in their very first project (as can you, and perhaps you did), but the process is difficult without guidance, time to learn, and time to correct mistakes. Seasoned professionals would quickly identify many of the challenges in Robin's situation and know of solutions and safeguards to apply. While even they might not suspect all the problems that may be encountered, the pros would often have effective means of dealing with them. Most novices would be taken off guard and flounder. Their projects might well fail painfully, if not irreparably. Not to worry.

Get your tux pressed

Your virtuoso performance is coming up! And your success is all about the process you use.

In this book, we're looking primarily at the process of e-learning design and development, because process is the key to navigating among and managing all the many tasks and potential problems every e-learning project has. We appropriately look at process first because process defines and constrains the activities that, in turn, determine the range of possible outcomes it can produce. In other words, process has a profound influence over the *quality*

Think

List at least three adjectives that would characterize the e-learning you think Robin's team produced.

of e-learning produced, not just its manageability—although some processes are clearly more manageable than others.

We're not actually going to delve into process management so much here, nor will we venture deeply into instructional design. Although we'll necessarily touch on both a bit, these are topics I intend to pick up elsewhere in this library.

Here, we'll stay focused on process, and we'll look at it from a new, refreshing, and decidedly pragmatic point of view. We'll examine successive approximation—a process that is in very successful use by many, but is radically different from what most have used in the past and still use (or claim to use) today. We'll examine both the pragmatic aspects of the process and its ability to support a wide range of learning theories.

Why a new process?

Because, frankly, the previously popular processes have produced disappointing results. Their disappointments have been many and diverse, including inconsistent or low product quality, team discord, poor speed of delivery, and high product cost. Produced applications have simply not realized enough

of the potential benefits e-learning offers. At conference after conference, I've asked attendees to give me a single adjective to describe e-learning—the first one that popped into their heads. The most frequent response: "Boring!" Most of the other responses haven't been any more favorable.

Think — Quick. What adjectives quickly come to mind when you think of being an e-learner?

Boring e-learning is bad e-learning. Ineffective e-learning. Expensive wasteful e-learning. Regrettable, damaging, useless e-learning. Bad, bad, bad.

If you should happen to wonder *why* boring is bad even though you surely know it instinctively, I'm really happy you're reading this book. Consider these observations:

➤ When learners are bored, you lose their attention. Since you can't learn for learners (they have to do the learning themselves), and since lack of attention blocks anything getting to learners' minds, learning doesn't happen. That's bad.

➤ When learners are bored by e-learning, they may conclude that they don't like e-learning. Of course, not all e-learning is boring. But first-time e-learners don't

33

know that and may think what they've experienced represents typical e-learning. They might then resist future involvement with e-learning—even well-designed e-learning that would be very helpful to them. That's bad.

➤ When learners are bored, they easily associate their negative experience with the subject being taught. Of course, the subject might be of great value to them and might be very interesting to them if only taught in a better way. But learners often root their attitudes based on initial experiences and never give themselves another chance. That's bad.

➤ When learners are bored, they are annoyed, even insulted by the organization that is ready to waste their time. They think neither their time, job, nor performance must be very important. This can lead to sloppy performance and high attrition levels. That's bad.

I'm sure you can add other reasons why boring e-learning is bad e-learning.

I make a point of this because, apparently, many organizations think boring e-learning is not so bad. They deploy much of it, often with a sense of great pride and high expectations. Maybe in their relief that they got it delivered, they don't see how boring their e-learning is from the learners' perspective. They see only a project completed. Success.

Maybe they don't realize how dynamic and effective e-learning can be. Maybe they don't know how to do anything else. Or maybe they think doing something more effective costs too much.

Frankly, I don't think it's a cost issue—or a staffing or resource issue, for that matter. Although many applications could clearly have been made better through greater financial investment, I think boring e-learning results from using outdated processes that focus on content presentation, accuracy, and comprehensiveness. And they result from using processes that rely too heavily on up-front analysis, that are often incomplete or inaccurate no matter how much time and effort are invested in it, and from using processes that don't provide key stakeholders a comfortable and effective way of being involved.

While content presentation, accuracy, and comprehensiveness are important things, throwing information at learners is rarely effective.

What we must do to change behavior is create learning experiences that maximize learner attention and cause learners to think and practice.

And while we don't expect operations managers to be instructional designers, relegating them to specification document approval and excluding them from goal definition and design exploration isn't smart. We need both their vision and knowledge as input just as much as they need to learn about the capabilities and alternatives that today's technology-assisted learning can provide. We need decision makers to understand what can be accomplished with various levels of investment, and to see that the most significant costs lie rarely in the development and delivery of effective learning experiences but rather in the costs of inadequately enabling people to perform.

How do process and product relate?

Can't we just use the old, and to many, the familiar processes, but redefine the targeted outcome by listing the characteristics of the e-learning product we want?

No, we can't. Process determines what happens, when it happens, and to what degree it happens. It reflects the values of the people who choose to use it and ultimately the characteristics of the end product.

A defined process is, in many ways, a detailed statement of what is important in the final product. If the process focuses on content organization, clarity, and structure, with multiple reviews by a panel of experts, then, clearly, content accuracy is a critical value. If the process requires multiple evaluations by and with learners, observes and discusses their reactions with them, and expects design modifications to occur based on learner responses, then we know that the learning experience is a primary value.

If the process includes no learning evaluation, then we know that the desired product is not so much learning but something else, probably budget compliance, schedule adherence, and problem avoidance. If the process includes learning posttests but no subsequent behavioral assessment, then we know that behavioral change was not really valued.

Process defines what we want and largely determines what we can actually get, whether we are cognizant of it or not. Of course, both content precision and learning experience effectiveness are important. All processes should verify both. Ability to deliver smoothly, on time, and within budget are important too. We must have the means of managing to our constraints. And we shouldn't forget learning and behavioral change. Remember what it was all about in the first place.

Seven Weaknesses in Typical e-Learning Design and Development Processes

Analysis	Design and Development	Evaluation
1. The learning/performance context determines needs and the range of solutions that can succeed, but typical processes prescript unrealistically comprehensive up-front analysis. Most teams respond by doing very little at all and fail to assess critical elements. 2. Few processes give formal recognition to the influence of political forces and structures within organizations, let alone define means of working with them. As a result, opportunities are missed, vital resources aren't made available, implementation support is lacking, and targets shift as players jockey their positions.	3. Specification documents and storyboards are ineffective ways of creating, communicating, and evaluating design alternatives. As a result, poor designs get pushed through the process and aren't recognized until too late. 4. Detailed processes become proceduralized and linear to the point that creativity becomes a nuisance. 5. The need to redesign and/or develop because better design ideas were discovered during development is considered a fault rather than an anticipated part of the process. As a result, teams are reluctant to recognize faults or question the quality of designs.	6. The only evaluation that really matters is whether new behaviors are actually enabled and exhibited. But in reality, almost no one measures such things to provide a feedback loop back to design. As a result, learning programs are designed to meet criteria that are measured (schedule, cost, throughput) and fail to focus on and achieve behavioral changes. 7. To say posttests are meaningless is only a mild overstatement, but if any learning measures are implemented, they are typically posttests. As a result, designs focus on preparing learners for excellent posttest performance that may not transfer to any valued behaviors at all.

You cannot optimize a process if you don't have established criteria for the product it must produce. And you can't get a great product with a process that is optimized for different purposes.

I can warm up my pizza in my microwave oven, but I get a soft, lifeless crust. I can't correct this by changing the amount of time I nuke the pizza. My problem, if I want my crust crispy on the bottom, is that I'm using the wrong process to heat the pizza. I need a fundamentally different process to achieve my desired goal.

Seven deadly sins

Disregard for the impact that process has on product characteristics has severely undermined the realized success of e-learning. Perhaps it's simply the deterministic force of tradition, belief that embedded processes are unimpeachable, or fear of risks in unknown approaches that has maintained the practice of producing suboptimal e-learning while vigorously defending the processes that produce it.

Applied processes have actually been weak in the beginning (analysis), the middle (design and development), and the end (evaluation), as

you can see from the table on page 36.

These seven weaknesses are undoubtedly responsible for our many failures to realize the greatest potential e-learning has to offer.

Successive approximation

The solution is a process that both owns up to past failures and addresses each one of these seven problem points head on. Feel free to jump to Chapter 6, wherein I begin detailing this process, which is covered throughout the remainder of this book. For those interested in considering the derivation of this process and its contrast to ADDIE, please read on.

Thanks, ADDIE

It makes intuitive sense to follow the ADDIE process of getting your Analysis done before you begin Design. And getting Design done before Development; Development before Implementation; and Implementation before Evaluation. Although there are almost as many adaptations of the process as there are instructional designers, making the precise definition of ADDIE something of a problem, the typical components and sequence of events

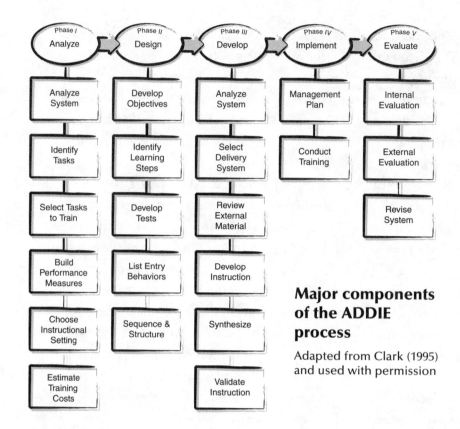

Phase I Analyze	Phase II Design	Phase III Develop	Phase IV Implement	Phase V Evaluate
Analyze System	Develop Objectives	Analyze System	Management Plan	Internal Evaluation
Identify Tasks	Identify Learning Steps	Select Delivery System	Conduct Training	External Evaluation
Select Tasks to Train	Develop Tests	Review External Material		Revise System
Build Performance Measures	List Entry Behaviors	Develop Instruction		
Choose Instructional Setting	Sequence & Structure	Synthesize		
Estimate Training Costs		Validate Instruction		

Major components of the ADDIE process

Adapted from Clark (1995) and used with permission

that comprise the process are shown above. There is much to be learned from studying, and even applying, the ADDIE process. The figure above shows only the higher-level steps that should be taken—or at least carefully considered in each phase of the process. Each step is then further broken down into substeps, each with specified criteria for completeness, accuracy, and quality.

For example, consider the development of objectives. A quality check is typically included to be sure each objective has all the required components, as shown in the flow diagram on the following page.

While no one supporting the use of behavioral objectives would argue that objectives shouldn't have the three criteria shown in the process figure and as taught to us by Robert Mager, these loops actually, and

Resource

🖳 Clark, D. (1995). See www. nwlink.com/~donclark/hrd/sat.html for a detailed presentation of the ISD/ADDIE model.

ironically, illustrate the linear basis of the phase-based process. That is, one attempts to perfect each piece of the design as one goes forward because the output of each step is input to the next. Again, the intent is to get it right so it doesn't have to be done over. Unfortunately, perfection at the micro level easily shifts focus away from the prime target at the macro level.

To be manageable, it's important to keep moving forward. Imagine how difficult it would be if one were to go back to the beginning of the process to see whether the output of each step necessitated the revision of any prior steps. If revisions were made, these revisions would then themselves require reevaluating their predecessors and so on. This would be an

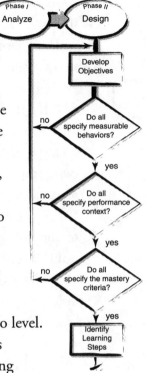

unmanageably iterative process.

It's understandable then why ADDIE managers generally insist on meticulously meeting applicable criteria at each step and moving forward. In general, going back to make changes is evidence that someone made a mistake. Someone either failed to meet the criteria or set some faulty criteria. Considering loop backs as unfortunate errors puts ADDIE managers at odds with their team and creates an atmosphere of tension—quite the opposite of the energetic, fun, and imaginative environment that more easily fosters the design of creative learning experiences.

The "new" ADDIE

Responding to the realities that few things are ever made to perfection, that waiting until everything is finished and integrated before commencing evaluation is waiting too long, and that experimentation is an essential process for discovery and invention, some have updated the

Resource

📖 *Preparing Instructional Objectives: A Critical Tool in the Development of Effective Instruction.* Robert F. Mager. (1997). Atlanta: CEP Press

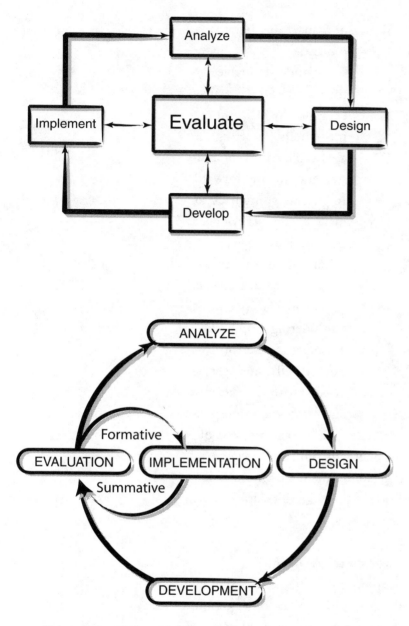

"New" ADDIE Models Move Toward Iteration

Top: An early, somewhat iterative adaptation by Control Data Corporation (corporate publication 7636827A, 1980)

Bottom: A "dynamic" model emphasizing frequent evaluation instead of phases (Clark, D. 1995)

ADDIE flow diagrams, as shown here.

This adaptation is an important step forward. Indeed, frequent evaluation is important, as the new ADDIE flow diagram imparts. Unfortunately, as soon as we begin asking specific questions, such as (with respect to just the analysis phase): How do you evaluate the analysis? Isn't activity design a method of evaluating the analysis? or How much analysis is enough?, we get very different answers from different practitioners. As one industry leader put it, "Apart from agreement that the process is generally one incorporating analysis, design, development, implementation, and evaluation, there's quite a bit of argument and disagreement" (Zemke & Rossett, 2002).

The many varying definitions of ADDIE one finds make its utility problematic. Which definition is the real definition? The right one? The best one? What version do we teach and apply? What do we really mean when we refer to ADDIE? Just saying it's a process that involves analysis, design, development, implementation, and evaluation isn't enough of a process definition to matter.

Resources

📖 Zemke, R. and Rossett, A. (2002). A Hard Look at ISD. Training. 39(2). 26-35.

💻 Saul Carliner. Unpublished paper, "An Instructional Design Framework for the Twenty-First Century." http://education.concordia.ca/~scarliner/idmodel.pdf

There has been much criticism of the process, and its justification has been made all the more tenuous because defenders frequently defend only "their" ADDIE process. Sometimes, even more problematically, its advocates point out that ADDIE really isn't a process per se, but is rather a conceptual framework intended merely to guide thinking and not to delineate step-by-step activities.

All this, unfortunately, weakens ADDIE further because, in this context, ADDIE becomes whatever a practitioner makes of it. It has multiple definitions, a fluid definition, or an obscure definition that's useful only in the hands of highly experienced professionals. Trying to refine or correct ADDIE at this point seems futile. Although Saul Carliner has prepared a very

thoughtful paper on how we might do just that, it seems like water over the dam at this point. If we contemplate going in this direction, I fear we won't know if one is using the "New" New ADDIE with or without modifications, or what.

What we need is a clearly differentiated and defined process that works—not necessarily a foolproof process that works in hands of novices, but at least a robust process that has a high probability of producing successful learning events when executed thoughtfully. We need a process that, when someone claims to be using it, we know at least what he or she is trying to do.

It's been good knowing you

In addition to being variably-defined and poorly understood, ADDIE just no longer keeps pace with alternatives available to us today. A workhorse since its development for the Joint Chiefs of Staff in the mid-1970s (Hannum, 2005), its

Resource

📖 Hannum, W. (2005, July-August). Instructional Systems Development: A 30 Year Retrospective. *Educational Technology*, 5-21.

purpose was to assist in the rapid development of military training, often by personnel with little background in instructional design.

Larger corporations adopted it and many universities taught this process, as did I. But technology has advanced, bringing about a broader array of learning event possibilities, together with heightened learner expectations and increased challenges to the instructional designer.

Designers can now use media to more fully address the whole learner, including not only their cognition but their emotions as well. Dramatic events can draw learners in, heighten their attention and interest, and motivate them to do their best, both while learning and afterward. With today's visual effects in movies and on television and with the familiar power of interactive electronic games, e-learning application designers must address a much richer array of technology-based elements if they are to win learner interest, respect, and engagement.

New tools, new futures

Thankfully, the advancement of technologies that press designers for more compelling elements has also introduced more powerful tools.

Development of interactivity, animation, 3-D graphics with subtle shading and translucency, synchronized sounds, precise time-based learner response analysis, and much more are not only possible, but are also components that can be developed quickly and within reasonable budgets.

Prototypes can be developed just to experiment. Major modifications can be made in the exploration of alternative designs. Functional models become development specifications that communicate by example, replacing easily misinterpreted specification documents.

These advances are more than nice-to-have utilities; they create new process possibilities. Seen in contrast to all this, ADDIE is now both an inefficient and insufficient process that too frequently and laboriously produces unsatisfactory, out-of-date results.

The same old problems

The problems we have in creating successful e-learning have unfortunately been with us since the pioneering efforts of the 1960s. Then, as now, it was difficult to develop an interactive experience that engaged the learner, optimized learner time, adapted to individual learner needs, and provided practice that created applicable skills.

Indeed, seasoned designers often comment that nothing seems to have changed, even with all the amazing technological advances surrounding and supporting e-learning today. The primary challenges in producing quality learning experiences really haven't changed much at all. Sure, we have networks, low-cost multimedia computers, and an enormous array of software tools; but it doesn't seem like we've made much progress in simplifying the design of great learning experiences.

I think the explanation for this isn't so obscure. We've stuck to the same process we had when the supporting hardware and software were in their infancy. It used to be important, for example, to give programmers a precise specification of what we wanted to have built, because making changes, sometimes even changes that appeared to be minor, often caused great setbacks to the programming. It wasn't possible to explore ideas and possibilities on the computer in real time, because of the time needed to implement them. That is one of the reasons ADDIE became what it did—a process that attempts to avoid making changes downstream.

Without being able to explore the impact of alternative design ideas, whether prohibited by technology or by the process you use, the design challenge is a tough one. Processes must adapt if we are to harness the aid that technology advances offer. Processes that not only adapt but also take full advantage of new possibilities will naturally offer the greatest benefits.

My purpose in this book is not to berate ADDIE (although I've not avoided it as much as I intended), its parent Instructional Systems Design (ISD), or its loyal proponents. Indeed, it has served as a helpful stepping-stone, and we have learned much from its use. Rather, I intend to share a more contemporary process that's actually the secret of success in use by many of today's award-winning designers and is proving to be much more effective across the board.

Time for something better

We have actually made significant progress against the primary challenge of more easily and reliably building great learning events, and, perhaps surprisingly, it does come in part from the technology itself. We now have new ways of evaluating designs in rapid succession with real learners. Despite the occasional, fascinating, but ultimately rhetorical argument that instructional design is a science, we know that creating effective learning experiences is a combination of art and process, of experimentation and application of principles, of creativity and diligence.

e-Learning both introduces new learning possibilities and makes greater demands on the development process. New learning possibilities include realistic simulations that have the appeal and energy of games and also build important skills useful in the real world. New learning possibilities that motivate learners to change what they've been doing, not just pass the posttest and return to old habits on the job. New learning possibilities that are so beneficial that learners will choose them over other learning opportunities open to them.

But fostering dynamic interactive learning experiences cannot be done using the same design and development process one would use to prepare a live presentation, to write a book, or to build a page-turning PowerPoint application. We need a process that recognizes that our work is a mixture of art and science. We need a process that is open for exploration where it needs to be and procedural where it needs to be. We need a process that's good up-front, in the middle, and at the end.

And finally, it's time to move our design process forward, to upgrade it for use with today's tools, delivery capabilities, and most importantly, with our improved understanding of how people learn in today's energetic, information-overloaded environment.

6 | Making Useful Mistakes (ASAP)

George, director of Zanick Pharmaceuticals' security training, was convinced he needed some quick demos to present and evaluate his ideas. He asked CLO Emily Hayes for an adept developer who could prototype some of the possible learning experiences he envisioned.

Emily was eager to see what George had in mind and wanted to support his zeal to get everything off to a quick start. She nearly agreed to let George get right into it. She was convinced the iterative design—prototype—evaluate process she had read about would flush out problems and opportunities efficiently, but something didn't seem quite right.

She wasn't thinking George would be wasting time. That wasn't it. But she was a bit concerned about her credibility with the organization if she appeared to be flailing around. Shouldn't there be a plan?

Getting ready to make mistakes

Emily was thinking right. She didn't want to make regrettable mistakes right out of the chute, but she almost leapt without looking.

A little preparation facilitates making useful mistakes and reduces the likelihood of wasting time floundering about. This is where Emily needs to start Zanick Pharmaceuticals—with a little data gathering and analysis that's sometimes called *backgrounding*.

Backgrounding

As we start out, we should first check those things that can help us make sure we'll be productive when we call our first team meeting. We can do this quickly, typically over a period of just a few days. Perhaps surprisingly, we'll focus more on getting the right people involved than on defining the content of the training. Iterative prototyping and evaluation cycles will help us gather and analyze missing information and even reassess whether the original targets are the right ones.

As we traverse the new process, we begin with data-gathering work that can be done

45

quickly. We emphasize anything we can do to determine who should participate in the iterative cycles we'll be doing next. The remaining data collection and analysis, we'll actually do in the iterative evaluations.

Let's look ahead a bit to see how we'll use the results of our backgrounding work by unveiling part of the successive approximation process diagram below. Then we'll return to backgrounding.

The heart of successive approximation is the design—prototype—review cycle that is repeated, usually about three times for each critical design, until the design meets established criteria and can serve as a basis for full development. These iterative cycles are quite amazing in their ability to flush out hidden information, create new insights, and bring about consensus. Their success is not dependent on much prior input but does require having the right people participating, and, of course, having the

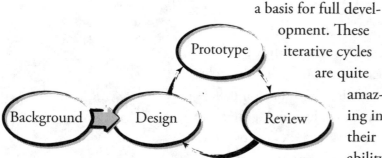

effective event leadership you will provide.

Top 10 backgrounding questions

Even though the necessary input from up-front analysis is minimal, it isn't nil. Some issues tend to become knotty, confusing, or worse if they catch you blindsided. It's best to do some research and preparation to make sure your design sessions will go well.

Here are ten questions that should be addressed before you begin the iterative prototyping cycles:

1. What business problem is being addressed (corporate) or what performance competencies are the target (academia)?
2. What behavioral outcomes are needed and how will you know whether you have achieved them?
3. Do learners lack the training or education necessary to perform, or are they not performing for other reasons?
4. What abilities do performers currently have?
5. What incentives and disincentives are in place for both desired performance and undesired performance?

6. Are needed tools and resources available and appropriately accessible for desired performance?

7. Who will be approving the resources to be applied in creating a solution (the decision-maker) and actually making them available?

8. Whose opinions does the decision-maker rely on?

9. Who directly supervises the people to be trained?

10. Who has profit-and-loss responsibility that's based most directly on the performance of the people being trained?

Let's look at the questions in detail to understand why each is pertinent and what we can hope to derive from asking it. We'll use Zanick Pharmaceuticals as an applied case study and example.

The goal questions

Questions 1 through 4 probe into the basic task at hand. The primary reasons for asking these questions at the start is to determine whether a well-founded instructional need exists and is identified similarly by all key players.

1. What business problem is being addressed (corporate) or what performance competencies are the target (academia)?

We need to be sure we know what problem we're trying to solve. The odds of hitting the bull's eye are much better if you know where the target is. Many things can cause us to be somewhat off in target identification at this early stage. Without deep thought, for example, key individuals can quickly scribble down a goal that really isn't what they want (or need). It might be all they think they can get, or they might confuse an enabling step with the ultimate goal.

George went to the head of security to get an idea of what would be the best content to develop for their reevaluation of e-learning project. He didn't want something that would be unreasonably challenging and therefore risk discrediting e-learning once again. But he did want something that would impress top management.

After a few minutes of head scratching, the head of security said she'd like managers to know the difference between harmless comments of frustration that workers make from time to time and com-

ments that represent a real threat to employee safety.

This sounded good to George, and he went off satisfied that he should build a program that taught verbal threat detection to managers.

Of course, knowledge of warning signs wasn't Zanick Pharmaceuticals' business. Manager knowledge of warning signs wouldn't bring in more revenue, reduce insurance costs, or even make the workplace safer—*unless* managers actually *acted* to make the workplace safer.

But what George learned was enough to set a general goal. It wasn't the "real" goal, and it would have sent an ADDIE user in the wrong direction, but this was close enough for the process we're going to discuss. To prevent consuming a tremendous amount of time and patience inefficiently fine-tuning, it's ok to work initially from a sense of where the target is without knowing the exact coordinates of the bull's eye. If you can be more exact, that's great. But don't fret if the target is a little loose. You'll zero in on it precisely a little later.

2. What behavioral outcomes are needed and how will you know whether you have achieved them?

"This should be a piece of cake," George told Emily. "I read that declarative knowledge is taught more effectively through e-learning than by live classroom instruction. (See resource below.)

"I'll get it to work and prove the value of e-learning. I'll build in a posttest, and the scores will tell us objectively whether managers know which employee statements are of concern and which ones are not."

George didn't get the needed behavioral outcomes from the head of security, although he thought he did. You see again, in truth, nobody cares what the managers know; they care what they do. The head of

Resource

Sitzmann, Traci M., Kraiger, K., Stewart, David W., & Wisher, Robert A. (no date). *The Comparative Effectiveness of Web-Based and Classroom Instruction: A Meta-Analysis.* Department of Defense contract number DASW01-03-C-0010. Download from: www.moresteam.com/ADLMeta-AnalysisPaper.doc

security confused what he saw as a necessary step toward the real goal of greater security and lower cost/risk operations as the goal itself.

Behavioral outcomes aren't knowing things, and the outcomes we need aren't posttest scores. Behavioral outcomes of interest are successful real-world performances.

3. Do learners lack the training or education necessary to perform or are they not performing for other reasons?

George asked Emily, but she didn't know why screening employee comments had become a concern. "I suppose you'll have to go back and ask the head of security again, but I hate to have you bother her too much. I'm funding this project, and she could mess it up by getting too involved and confusing things."

George started walking back to the security office, but decided to heed Emily's warning and went to HR instead. Although he didn't find answers there, they showed him an easy way he could do a survey through e-mail and the Internet. He could easily select employees by position, post a few questions, and have the results tabulated automatically.

So George asked all company managers whether they felt confident in recognizing security threats in day-to-day communications. He also asked those who have managers reporting to them whether they felt their managers would recognize such security threats.

Surveys, interviews, and e-mail are some easy and often-effective ways of getting some data that you might have thought were hard to gather. Focus groups can also generate valuable information if you have the skill to conduct them and can get the needed resources and participation.

4. What abilities do performers currently have?

Through his electronic surveys, George learned that managers were pretty sure they could handle most any situation themselves, but they weren't so sure about the subordinate managers they supervised. In the open comments area of survey responses, a number of managers expressed surprise that they had any responsibility for risk detection and management. Some flatly stated that they were much too busy to even think about this, let alone take training on it.

This was important information that George and Emily needed. It's likely there really is a performance problem, because managers weren't even aware of their responsibilities here. It's not likely that just calling this responsibility to the attention of managers will change behavior as needed, although sometimes that does work. Because of the subtleties of risk detection and liabilities in handling of delicate employee situations, Zanick managers needed training.

The context questions

Questions 5 and 6 probe into the basic task at hand and find out how much contextual work will be necessary for the development of learning events and to ensure their success in application.

5. What incentives and disincentives are in place for both desired performance and undesired performance?

George found HR to be very helpful again. From records he discovered there, he noted that few managers actually attended the security training that was offered annually. Most managers had skirted the "requirement" every year.

The Managers' Handbook *did contain guidelines on detecting and handling security risks, but there was no formal check to see whether managers actually read and understood them, let alone put them into practice.*

There are many determinants of human behavior. Some are obvious, many are subtle, while others are ignored. If something is a lot of effort, for example, and no one seems to care, then why not skip it and do things that garner rewards?

6. Are needed tools and resources available and appropriately for desired performance?

It appears that Zanick had guidelines for managers that would have been an important resource if managers used them. But managers lacked awareness of their responsibilities as well as perhaps the time necessary for actually taking the responsibility. Time, of course, is a necessary resource to perform additional behaviors.

The who's who questions

Questions 7 through 10 help identify the people who really should participate in defining the project and getting it started in the right direction. Getting the right answers to these questions is the most important backgrounding activity. If you get this correct, then any errors made in answering the other questions can be corrected when the leadership team works through the iterative design—prototype—review cycles.

7. Who will be approving the resources to be applied in creating a solution (the decision-maker) and actually making them available?

The answer to this question might be complex, and it might be very hard to get, but it's very important to find out who really has responsibility and resources for an effective solution.

Come out, come out, wherever you are! It's not unusual for the people holding the ultimate decision-making responsibility to hide. The reasons for this problematic behavior vary, but often it's simply because decision-makers are so busy. They need to delegate as many responsibilities as possible.

Executives often have reservations about the value of training and sometimes keep them to themselves.

They may support training more because it's a logical activity than because they truly believe in its effectiveness.

Alternatively, executives may feel that they're simply out of their area of competence or comfort. Executives rarely get to top positions because of their success in implementing training programs (although their leadership coaching skills may well have had something to do with it). Most likely, it was because of their sales or operational management skills that advance them on the corporate ladder. They're unfamiliar with the learning field's lingo and even the fundamental concepts. Participation could be embarrassing.

The person at the top has budget-making authority (or he or she wouldn't be at the top). You would really like to have this person participating in the iterative design process because he personally will see the possibilities that emerge from the process. The possibilities might include tackling a broader range of business needs or, conversely, focusing more deeply on a few behaviors that, through the iterative design—prototype—review process, become recognized as a bigger problem and opportunity. Or it might make sense to reduce the scope of the entire project and extend the timeline to implement a trial application before gambling more of the company's resources.

Sometimes, resources are approved at the top but not actually made available due to other commitments or lack of support by management or the organization. Unfortunately, it's not enough to know who's in charge of the money. You also have to know who's in charge of the people you need and whether that person will provide the needed personnel when you need them. This can be sensitive territory, especially if you're an outside consultant. So tread carefully, but try your level best to find out.

8. Whose opinions does the decision-maker rely on?

For so many reasons when it comes to deciding how they spend their time, executives often delegate learning development directives to the fullest extent they can. They aren't personally and seriously investigating all the ways that training might address their performance problems (probably no one is). The stated challenges are probably, how can we get the costs down, deliver it sooner, and teach it faster?

You need to get them involved in order to influence their thinking and earn their support.

9. Who directly supervises the people to be trained?

So often overlooked is the rich source of information that the trainees' supervisor is. Supervisors know the individual strengths and weaknesses of their people and the effects they have. They should also be able to tell you what prevents their crews from accomplishing identified goals.

Regardless of how perceptive they may be, we want a representative supervisor to be very much involved in the process of inventing a performance training solution. We need both whatever insights she has and, perhaps most important, her support in helping learners transfer their new abilities to actual on-the-job performance.

10. Who has profit-and-loss responsibility that's based most directly on the performance of the people being trained?

Although all of top management cares about performance, there's usually someone with direct responsibility for both the behavioral performance of concern and the profit-and-loss performance. Of all those we can identify, this person may have the most to gain from a spectacular learning application, the most ability to help a project succeed, and the easiest means of ruining it.

If at all possible, we want this person involved in the earliest iterative work—and usually for as long as he or she is willing and able to participate.

Gathering critical information

Remember, getting ready for the iterative process can be a relatively quick step. It isn't necessary to gather the detailed opinions of key people; rather, we are more concerned about identifying those people who can make or break the success of the project and securing their participation. We don't want these people digging their heels in to defend a position taken too soon, so we won't ask questions that might result in position statements. We just want to know who's who.

Even though we actually want to be open to a shift in focus—as we may well find to be appropriate in the iterative work we are about to

do—we need to identify the problem that initiated the project and do so as early as possible, not because we wouldn't welcome a shift to a different set of behaviors or even to a different set of learners if that turned out to be a better opportunity, but because identifying a problem helps us identify the key people we need to work with. We can also begin asking meaningful questions about what relevant resources are available, both human and material, when we know this. We can do some study of the content so that we can use at least some of the terms and concepts without having to ask for a translation of every statement. And we can ask about current and previous attempts, if any, to teach the targeted behaviors.

If we see respondents differing with each other, that's ok. It's typical, actually, and one of the reasons the process has evolved to the point of requiring an assembly of key people for the initial iterative work. Even when respondents don't appear to differ with each other at first, we expect important differences to emerge shortly after the process begins.

Remember, we want to identify multiple points of view and make sure that our clients also recognize their variances at a point in the process where these variances are helpful for brainstorming and considering alternatives. We don't want to put off dealing with substantive variances until later when we no longer have time or resources to explore various options.

Resource

⌨ Download sample reports from the backgrounding efforts of real projects at www.alleninteractions.com/books/background.htm. These reports differ in style and content, yet both were successful in preparing the team for the next phase of activities. For your first successive approximations project, you might use one of them as a model to guide you, after which you'll be ready to draft your own set of process aids.

Working with backgrounding information

We complete backgrounding not to get a good grade or comply with my recommendations, but rather to conduct productive work sessions and thereby to succeed in the following steps. Writing up your findings is a valuable thought exercise as well as a means of preparing a document that can be a valuable tool.

What if there's no agreement on the primary goal (Question 1)?

You could throw your hands up in frustration and invite them to call you when they knew what they wanted to do. Or you could see this as a major opportunity to help the organization come together on a plan.

If you take the latter approach, your only significant problem at this point is knowing whom to invite to your rapid prototyping sessions. You'll have to use your intuition here, but it's probably wise to take guidance from the person who controls the budget and has direct profit-and-loss responsibility. As the team works together, they may change the target learner group or the behaviors being developed. If so, it's important progress, and you may need to respond by reconstituting the rapid prototyping team. Be thankful this course correction happened early in the process.

What if no one can define success (Question 2)?

This is bad news, although it's not at all atypical for organizations to have little interest in actually measuring the impact of learning applications. It's bad news because it probably indicates that the learning envisioned has no direct connection to a defined business need or an identified behavioral outcome. This, in turn, means the project may actually have little prospect of success—especially if, later on, someone decides to question it.

Note this concern and prepare to talk about the importance of having measurable criteria for success established at the outset. You'll also want to be prepared to reject posttest scoring as a means of evaluating the project's success (except for applications designed to prepare learners to pass certification tests or other tests. You want measures of meaningful behavioral change.

What if learners don't lack needed skills (Question 3)?

It's often assumed that lack of desired behavior is caused by a lack of ability. Many times it isn't the lack of ability that's determining what people choose to do. Level of effort, recognition and reward, availability of resources, and competing time demands are just a few of the factors that are often affecting behavior.

Here you'll need to determine what factors are influencing behavior and determine what can and should

be done about them. It could still be that learning interventions are needed, but it might be time management training that's the best solution. Perhaps supervisors need training on providing more effective rewards for desirable performance or on resource scheduling.

What if performers have very different levels of proficiency (Question 4)?

It's a big problem when people enroll in learning programs that are beyond their readiness level or too elementary for them. And, of course, the cost of developing programs that accommodate a wide range of entry skills is much higher than developing them for a more homogeneous group.

Nevertheless, individual variance is one of the important justifications for e-learning and blended learning programs. For example, e-learning, with its ability to adapt to learner needs and provide varying amounts of practice as required to bring each learner up to standard levels of proficiency, is often used prior to group-based learning.

As long as the number of learners to be taught is large enough to justify the construction of variance-accommodating learning applications, the technology has excellent capacity to provide an effective and efficient solution.

What if there are incentives for undesired behavior (Question 5)?

First of all, don't be shocked. Confusing incentives and misperceived expectations just aren't all that unusual. There might not be incentives for desired behavior, and there well could be disincentives for desired behavior that have gone undetected. This will remind you how important it is to involve recent learners in the process. They may be able to explain what actually drives their behavior in ways no one else in the organization can.

You and your design team may decide that, instead of applying learning interventions, a change in the incentives program should be tried first. The answer to Question 3 will be helpful in determining your strategy.

What if tools and resources aren't available (Question 6)?

Again, don't be too surprised. Such situations sometimes aren't reported, and management can be unaware of the problem. There might not

be enough phone lines, supplies might take too long to requisition, knowledgeable people might be overbooked.

Again, talking to performers ahead of your team meetings can give you important insights and prepare you to lead discussions on sensitive issues that might not otherwise come up. A red flag here would suggest doing some additional data gathering before you risk igniting an uncomfortable and unproductive confrontation. Realize, however, that by discovering this problem, you can help an organization identify the real problem and thereby avoid spending time and effort developing solutions that couldn't do any good.

What if the real decision-maker isn't identified (Questions 7, 8, and 10)?

The person having profit-and-loss responsibility isn't usually hard to identify. This person is likely to be the primary decision-maker, but it isn't always the case, and there isn't always a P&L context. The project may be a human resources project undertaken in compliance with state law, for example. Or it might be development undertaken by an academic or charitable institution.

Not clearly identifying the ultimate decision-maker is a concern, make no mistake about it. It's not unusual for those with ultimate authority to wait in anonymity and see what others do, especially when training is a foreign topic to them, as it is to many leaders.

If the work doesn't look like it's going in the "right" direction, they issue directives to rectify the situation. Although these directives may reveal a key business vision or strongly held preferences about training, they come painfully late when issued as a corrective action. They may reveal only part of the information the team needs to construct a satisfactory design, resulting in further directives. And finally, by issuing directives rather than participating in a well-rounded consideration of the issues, top decision-makers can preclude an optimal strategy that would have come from open discussions and collaborative exploration.

So you really need to identify the top decision-maker. And you need to try everything you can manage to get the real decision-maker to participate in the initial rapid-prototyping activities.

If you're having trouble, try these techniques:

1. Have a small meeting that involves only top people. Executives are sometimes uncomfortable outside their normal sphere of day-to-day interactions. Here you can go over exactly what happens in rapid-prototyping sessions, explain how this is the most efficient way to get the organization on the right track, and discuss what happens when top people don't attend.

2. If you can't get a meeting together, individually ask each of those people you think might be the real decision-maker what he or she will do if there are important opportunities in the project that would require additional funding. "Hypothetically, what if you saw a way to do something really important in this project that wasn't foreseen. It could be, for example, something that would make a lot of money or spread your investment much further, increasing your ROI. What would you do?"

If your decision-maker candidate says he would have to get a budget increase approved, you know he isn't the real decision-maker. If the candidate says she'd consider making the funds available, you probably have your decision-maker. Whatever answers you receive will probably help you identify who is really in charge.

Much easier is identifying the people the top person trusts—the ones who can influence pretty much everything. Although many in the organization will claim they are the trusted ones, this shouldn't mislead you. Leaders will often tell you straight out, so be sure to inquire about who the leader trusts.

Influencers can wreak havoc on projects in much the same way that lie-in-wait decision-makers do. By not participating and voicing their viewpoints up-front, influencers can stir things up late in the process. Sometimes they do this indirectly,

which is usually worse, by riling up the key decision-maker, who then redirects a project abruptly. If the results are still not as hoped, the masked influencers may resort to even more devious and scurrilous methods.

None of these problems is to be expected, but they are far too frequent for you not to preclude them to the best of your ability. Again, the challenges to achieving an excellently designed learning application are many. It's important that we use a process that recognizes the real-world challenges that exist and addresses them flat-out. We mustn't bury ourselves in the principles of human learning, instructional design, and user interface while ignoring the contextual issues that must be aligned to support our success.

7 | Inalienable Risks

Jim attended a national conference on e-learning and heard some pretty impressive statistics about sales increases achieved through better online training. As he listened to the details of projects, he felt certain his company didn't have the internal resources to undertake a successful e-learning project, so he hired a consulting firm to develop custom applications for Step Up Ladders.

He felt that a sharply targeted approach would be smart—nothing too ambitious, yet a project well positioned to achieve measurable results. The consultants from Learn-Some impressed Jim with the number of projects they had done and the depth of their skills.

A typical scenario

Carol Swanson of LearnSome asked Jim to schedule time to respond to a rather lengthy needs questionnaire her company used to assess the situation, propose a plan, and set a budget. Jim looked at the questions and, although he could answer some of them, he thought this wasn't really worth his time. He just wanted some effective training that would help his distributor network increase their sales. After all, their products were made much better than any equivalently priced competitor's. Jim sent Carol to his marketing director for answers.

Carol was very pleased with the detailed answers she received. She gleaned the following information from the carefully considered answers:

➤ *Step Up salespeople, of whom there are about 120, sell only to distributors and provide the primary channel of product information.*

➤ *Distributors are located in fourteen countries and speak six different languages, although all but two are comfortable with English.*

There are many, many ways for an e-learning project to go wrong. Three common, detrimental, but avoidable errors are:

1. Focusing on the solution and neglecting the problem

2. Treating e-learning as an expense

3. Delegating participation in a process that operationally defines the organization's vision

| How should an organization determine what to spend on a performance solution? | Think |

➤ In total, their distributors represent about 2,200 salespeople who, in turn, sell to about 7,700 retailers who have many on-floor salespeople.

➤ Salespeople increasingly service their clients through e-mail. All Step Up salespeople have computers, as do nearly all of their distributors.

➤ Salespeople congregate once every other year for a combination of training and performance recognition.

➤ Salespeople are continually asking for more aids, more events, more promotions, and any other assistance they can get.

➤ There are nine product lines. Four constitute the base Step Up product line, having from four to twenty products each. The remaining five product lines are private label products that are customized and feature client logos.

➤ Marketing literature compares the company's product lines in detail with each other and about six competitive brands.

➤ The sales organization has sales scripts that provide guidance, although they are not intended to be used verbatim.

Setting the budget?

One thing Carol couldn't deduce was how much money Step Up wanted to spend on their training. It's always a delicate situation. If LearnSome took into account the amount of information to be presented and used a rule of thumb of about three interactions per content point, she could calculate a cost and schedule. But they could always do something for more or less.

If they went in with a price that was much more than Step Up wanted to pay, she might lose the project opportunity. If she went in with less, well, money would be left on the table. So she really wanted to know the expectation.

Throwing out hints and subtle questions just wasn't working, so she asked Jim straight out what he expected to spend.

"I thought you'd tell me what my costs would be," he fired back. "I mean, I have no idea. I guess I was thinking maybe $35,000."

"I'm sure we can do something for $35,000," Carol said. She was *hoping to land a $50,000 account, but anything over $25,000 was of interest. She could probably come in with a bid of something close to $40,000 and sell it. That became her plan going forward.*

At random moments during the next few days, Jim would reflect on his budget discussion with Carol. Something was wrong.

"I gave her a number that would be a comfortable expenditure," he thought. "But is this what I should spend? Is there a correlation between cost and benefit?"

He phoned Carol and asked, "What should I be spending on this project, in your professional opinion? I just told you what I was expecting to spend, but I'm not sure if I'm spending enough or too much."

"You're just fine, Jim," came the reassuring reply. "This number is good for starters. I'm still working out the project plan and, in my analysis, I'll see whether we can get that number down or if we will really need to go up a bit. But I'm quite sure we're close to a good number."

"Ok, then. That's good. I'm glad I called. Let me know when we can review your plan and get going."

Hoodwinked

Jim's subconscious is smarter than he is. He was feeling uneasy about the process here, but he couldn't quite figure out what was wrong. With a lack of confidence from inexperience in training, he didn't push back. He didn't probe for information he really needed about what he'd lose if he spent less or what he'd gain if he spent more.

Jim is a smart guy, and you may be thinking that he'd ask some questions that seem obvious to you, especially if you have experience in training development. But the reality is that, when it comes to training, there's a mystique of terms, concepts, and processes that keeps sojourners like Jim apprehensive and not asking the prime questions.

Training talk

When Carol got back to Jim, she laid out her conclusions and draft plan. Carol used a beautifully designed PowerPoint presentation and provided handsome hardbound copies. The outline of her plan to train people on comparative ladder features is abstracted for you to review on the following pages.

> **Think** — What questions should Jim be asking?

Excerpts from LearnSome's Project Plan: Custom e-Learning for Step Up Ladders

1.0 The goal

The goal is to increase sales of ladders.

2.0 The solution

To increase ladder sales, buyers at retail stores need to know the differences between Step Up's product and other ladders. Because we can't train them directly, the distributors' salespeople need to know the differences themselves and convey this information to the buyers.

3.0 The targeted trainees

About 2,200 distributor salespeople would need training. Most speak English and have easy computer access.

4.0 The content

Sales literature itemizes the differences between each Step Up product and the top competing products. Having this content already developed greatly simplifies the project and makes both quantifying the work and laying out the schedule very straightforward.

5.0 The design

After a "glamour" opening, featuring upbeat music and an animated presentation of top-of-the-line Step Up Ladders, the application will present a concise listing of Step Up Ladder features in comparison to other products. Learners will be able to review and even select products to compare.

A game will make the lessons energetic and engaging. A bingo card will show a matrix of ladder features. Columns will represent different ladders. The first column will always be for a Step Up product, while the other four columns will each be labeled for one competing product. Each row will be labeled for a product feature.

Learners will select a square and then indicate whether the particular ladder has the feature named. If they were correct, they would "win" the square. If not, they would lose the square and any chance to bingo on any horizontal, vertical, or diagonal line that required the square.

Learners will be required to get five bingos before going on to a final posttest.

6.0 Performance measurement

All learners will be given a final posttest. Results will be collected in a simple centralized database that HR could access. It will list each employee who signed onto the training site, together with his or her posttest score.

7.0 The schedule

Deliverable/Milestone	Responsibility	Completion Date
Today's meeting	LearnSome	05/02
Approve plan	Step Up	05/04
Approve budget	Step Up	05/04
Sign contract	Both	05/11
Approve content	Skip step, available in product literature	
Present storyboard designs	LearnSome	06/01
Present revised storyboard designs	LearnSome	06/13
Approve storyboard designs	Step Up	06/13
Delivery of Alpha product	Step Up	08/01
Alpha review complete; comments documented	Step Up	08/09
Revised Alpha product delivered	LearnSome	08/26
Pilot starts	Step Up	08/26
Pilot complete; comments/problems documented	Step Up	09/03
Delivery of Beta	LearnSome	10/14
Beta review complete; comments documented	Step Up	10/21
Delivery of Gold Master (Final Application)	LearnSome	10/30

8.0 Change orders

Changes made after approval has been given will sometimes change the scope of the project, the total amount of work needed, or the dates on which subsequent deliverables can be provided. While LearnSome provides contingencies for such changes in planning, it's important that everyone agree that changes requested after approval may require a modification to the plan and/or budget.

9.0 The budget

A categorized budget was provided. Major items were:

Opening sequence (design and programming)	$ 3,200
Content presentation (80 products x 2 screens each)	$ 6,400
Bingo style game shell	$ 6,000
Content insertion into game shell (approx. 20 bingo cards)	$ 2,000
Posttest content development	$ 2,800
Use of proprietary posttest shell (perpetual license)	$ 3,500
Use of learner registration and completion data shell (annual license, 1st yr.)	$ 4,800
Quality assurance	$ 4,250
Management and planning	$ 8,200
Project total	$ 41,150

Any questions?

After her presentation, Carol paused for questions.

Jim sure liked the idea of having a sexy opening. He envisioned his best ladder being animated through all its configurations. He told Carol he'd really like to see some translucency so you could see the safety latches working as the ladder was raised and lowered. Carol assured him they planned to contract with one of the area's top animator/illustrators, who could do almost anything he could imagine.

Jim's excitement stayed in the stratosphere as he mused about all the product information becoming available online. Then he frowned as he wondered whether people would be able to find information on specific products without having to page through them all. He asked Carol about it.

"No problem," said Carol. "We'll make it easy to read through all the information consecutively, as well as to click items on a master list and go directly to them. We'll include photos of every product. Frankly, it will be easier to get this information into our training program than it currently is on your Web site, Jim."

Without really processing the annoying implications of this, Jim raced on. "I think your bingo game is a cool idea. Maybe even people who aren't into ladders will have fun with it and get interested in our products!" dreamed Jim. "It's got to be really easy to use, of course. I can't see our typical trainee being someone who's into those computer games kids play. Those games just seem so complicated unless you grew up with them."

"We'll lay it all out for you on our storyboards, Jim. You can see how it will work at a very detailed level before we start programming."

Jim hesitated. He wasn't sure he'd know what to do with storyboards, but it sounded simple enough, and he knew he shouldn't be trying to design training anyway. His day-to-day responsibilities were coming back to him.

"Well, I think I'll bow out of this project once we have our contract in place. I'm really not a judge of either training or computer software. Frankly, while this has been fun, I'm way out of my league here. I'm going to assign this project to a really sharp guy I've got in customer service. You'll like him.

"He's a computer wiz and he knows our product line inside and out. Your team and he should be a perfect match.

"I'll let him know what we've discussed and what I'm hoping to see happen here, but you work with him. Let's make this a big success!"

Carol thought this was great and thanked Jim in her charismatic manner for the business opportunity. Because Jim hadn't really questioned the budget, she was riding high. What a great day!

Process-inflicted damage

What happened? There are so many unfortunate but typical problems here. Here's a short list:

1. The budget was based on arbitrary cost expectations and expense comfort.
2. The budget was also based on a premature notion of content magnitude.
3. The proposed design focuses on electronic information publishing and product knowledge, not on building successful sales performance.
4. The discussion lost vision of the primary goal and took up elective topics, such as translucent graphics.
5. The key business leader—the person with performance responsibility—delegated involvement.

Expense vs. investment. To get it right, optimizing the budget for the greatest return, budgets should be set and accounted for from the perspective of an investment, not an expense. Jim's consultant should have helped him with this, because the two perspectives can lead thinking and action along very different paths.

Expenses are minimized, but investments are optimized for return. Investments are seen as having long-term benefits, usually reaching beyond the current fiscal year. They are amortized over time, protected, and supported. Expected returns are identified, forecast, and measured. (Echols, 2005).

Since what people learn doesn't evaporate at the close of the fiscal year and benefits can be long lasting, especially when continuing support is provided, just as is done for capital investments such as buildings or equipment, developing learning applications should be viewed and treated as an investment.

The budget presentation should have included a discussion of possible revenue gains, performance incentive programs, supervision training, and many other elements instead of merely an affordable cost.

Resource

Echols, M.E. (2005). *ROI on Human Capital Investment* (2nd ed.). Arlington, TX: Tapestry Press.

The project vs. the solution. The VP of Sales was caught up in novelty and imagination. He stepped out of the real world and his primary responsibilities at a critical moment. His e-learning provider was happy to respond to any expressed interest and support. She didn't remind Jim of the project's primary objectives and focus on measures of success. Rather than guiding her client in ways that might assure his success, she took the easy and all-too-typical path. LearnSome focused on the project, not the business solution.

While the process LearnSome used won a contract for them, it was almost certain to produce a disap-pointing and ineffectual learning application unless they circled back around to the business objectives.

It's true, many of us get side-tracked when an interesting, but tangential issue is raised. Jim wanted to be sure e-learning was going to be effective and cut his costs, but then he almost completely lost sight of that as he began to ponder a glamor-ous presentation of his products. It's all too easy to become excited about designing a game, using some fascinating imagery, or building some unique application and forget the primary goal.

We might have expected Jim to scoff at the glitz and push his big questions:

➤ How can we state the training goal in business terms?
➤ What's a reasonable ROI target?
➤ How will success be measured?
➤ Where's the sweet spot with respect to spending and benefit?

Balancing appeal, learning effective-ness, and costs is really the process challenge. The most desirable process will recognize our natural tendencies to focus on one or two of these and neglect the third. It will help us keep balance. It will also help us deal effectively with the complexities of the relationships among the key people who must guide the effort.

Process-guided success

I imagine you would agree with me that the process we want can guide us toward successful solutions. A process isn't successful if it just gets something done, whether within budget and schedule or not. More specifically, our process should:

➤ Help us determine the optimal amount to invest
➤ Help tackle the problem that is causing the greatest impediment to success
➤ Prevent seduction by fascinating media or interactivity that makes little contribution relative to its cost
➤ Keep us focused on the primary problem and behavioral solutions
➤ Keep the investor/buyer comfortably involved and in control, as appropriate
➤ Expedite completion of a solution in minimal time
➤ Keep costs as low as possible

You now appreciate the complexity of the task at hand, understand why typical processes fail, and recognize the very real-world issues the process must handle, in addition, of course, to all the technical and learning design issues.

With all this prerequisite understanding as a background, you're ready to appreciate the extraordinary value of successive approximation—an approach that does, indeed, do well against all these challenges. It's not an automatic process, of course. It takes leadership and skill to employ it effectively. But you can do it. Whether you're leading the process or just participating, we'll show you how to get the e-learning you want in Part Three.

Part Three

Applying Successive Approximation

The shortest distance isn't always a straight line.
It's Sunday afternoon, 1959. As usual, we pile into our Buick Special sedan, the four of us. My sister and I ride in the back, of course. Dad drives out into the Iowa countryside while Mom begins her random navigation.

"Let's see, we turned east last time. Let's go west. How many miles, kids? Pick a number from one to ten."

And so we began our attempt to get as lost as possible—to find spaces we'd never seen before and, if at all possible, to completely lose sense of direction. As we continued random turns, we'd look for things of interest. Sometimes we'd find a park, a peculiar old building, unfamiliar flowers, a malt shop, or a secluded lake.

Being entirely open to discoveries and having no particular agenda to promote often helped us create an experience that was better than any we could have planned. We learned. We played. Some discoveries were good for one trip—others just too compelling not to revisit later.

How do you design learning experiences—really effective learning experiences?

Producing learning applications of any significance within an organization's constraints requires a process. There are many interdependent components to design and build, and there are many types of criteria to meet. Time and money need to be spent wisely. A team usually undertakes the effort, and work needs to be coordinated. Timely communication is essential. And so on.

Setting the complex project management issues aside to address in another book, we still need an efficient process that is not only attuned to manageability, speed, and costs but also to the needs of learners and the performance success of the organization. We don't simply want to produce e-learning; we want to produce e-learning that is engaging, effective, and fun.

Why settle for anything less? We know from case studies that it's all possible.

While almost any process has a chance of succeeding on all fronts if given enough time and resources, I've sought a process that efficiently and reliably gives me e-learning solutions that are, in the words of Minnesota's Garrison Keillor, "strong, good-looking, and above average." While not perfect by any means, successive approximation is just such a process. Having worked and reworked it for decades, it is now very successful for me, for the studios in my company, and for e-learning developers around the world.

Chapter 8 – Successive Approximation Overview

This is a process overview, showing how successive approximation is actually a simple model that promotes creative design, identifies and corrects mistakes as early as possible, and expedites development.

Chapter 9 – Preparing for a Savvy Start

Rapid prototyping is fun and productive, as long as everyone focuses on the same objective and avoids getting bogged down in details. Here we discuss what you need to know and to get ready for the project kickoff.

Chapter 10 – Project Kickoff

You've prepared for the event and assembled the team. Following your agenda, your first task is to separate participants from their preconceptions as you create a team effort to identify the organization's primary learning goals and real opportunities for the project.

Chapter 11 – Rapid Design, Prototyping, and Evaluation

This is truly the fun stuff. It's brainstorming with the opportunity to see ideas become functional in a very short amount of time.

Chapter 12 – The Objectives x Treatments Matrix

As the Savvy Start process continues, insights are funneled into a few key design documents, such as the Objectives x Treatments Matrix, that are to become the project's foundation. As the team starts to understand in detail what needs to be done, objectives can be listed and prototyped designs can be assigned to them.

Chapter 13 – Assessing Context and Constraints

In the final phase of the Savvy Start, we need to direct the group's creative enthusiasm to the realities of their environment and budget. It's important that expectations align with reality at this point and that the group is unified in what they hope to see realized by the time the project is finished.

Chapter 14 – Completing Design, Planning Development

It's time to pause a moment and produce a comprehensive plan based on an analysis of the Savvy Start, the Objectives x Treatments Matrix, and the prototypes. With approval of the plan, budget, and schedule, we can return to iterative cycles to complete the design.

Chapter 15 – Develop— Implement—Evaluate

There's a good deal more work to do, but the process will feel familiar. A series of iterative development cycles, each with a specific purpose and set of evaluation criteria, produces the final "golden" application release.

In This Part

8 | Successive Approximation Overview

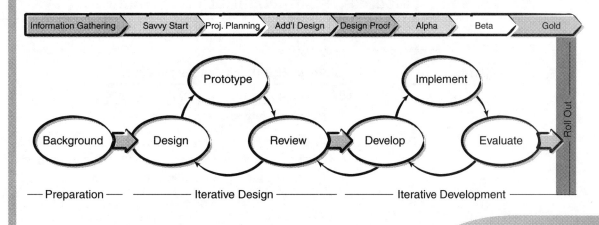

| Information Gathering | Savvy Start | Proj. Planning | Add'l Design | Design Proof | Alpha | Beta | Gold |

Prototype

Implement

Background → Design → Review → Develop → Evaluate → Roll Out

— Preparation — — Iterative Design — — Iterative Development —

Successive approximation is a successful process for the design and development of e-learning because it is practical, manageable, double-checks assumptions, promotes creativity, communicates effectively, involves all key stakeholders, and aligns solutions to needs. That's a lot. But at its heart, it's a very simple, iterative process that's repeatedly applied to a carefully defined sequence of issues.

For context and perspective, let's take a quick tour of the overall process and then focus on each component in detail in the remaining chapters. Activity descriptions begin on the next page.

The overview diagram above shows how the process begins after backgrounding with the Savvy Start exercise and concludes with the delivery of the final or "gold" product.

The process is divided into only three phases, Preparation, Iterative Design, and Iterative Development. Iterative cycles are used both in design and in development work to confirm the desirability of what was done and make corrections. Changes are expected with decreasing significance

�>apid reader

- Successive approximation is a simple, iterative process that achieves the best solution within given constraints.

- Successive approximation repeats design, development, and evaluation to work systematically toward the goal.

- Quality assurance is performed throughout the process.

Successive Approximation Activities

Phase/Activity	Function/Description
Preparation	**Determine key factors for success**
Backgrounding	• First primary objective: Identify key players and get their commitment to participate
	• Key players: Decision/budget-maker, opportunity-owner, subject expert, performance supervisor, recent learner, target learner, organization's project manager
	• Second primary objective: Identify business opportunity and its dependency on behavioral change
	• History: What performance enhancement efforts have been tried in the past? What programs are currently in use? What content materials are available?
	• Speed: This work is done quickly.
Iterative Design	**Create initial designs in Savvy Start as the basis for project planning.**
	Additional iterative design work, if needed, is completed after the project plan is approved.
Savvy Start: Design—Prototype—Review (rapid prototyping cycles)	• Participants: Key organization players (listed above), event leader (you?), instructional designer, prototyper(s)
	• Iterative cycles are used to witness and evaluate the direction suggested by gathered information, assumptions, and early ideas.
	• Prototypes are very rough and finished just barely enough to communicate and test ideas.
	• Outcome objectives are listed, along with the prototyped designs that will be used to help learners achieve them.
	• Review is done merely by discussion. Defining and changing everything, even the business problem to be addressed and the people to be trained, may be appropriate.
	• Again, rapid is the key word.

Project Planning	• Based on the designs created and/or selected in the Savvy Start, it's now possible to create a project plan that has integrity.
	• The first step is to capture directions set or suggested by preparing and circulating a Savvy Start Summary Report.
	• Initial media and content style guides can also be prepared, although they are likely to be incomplete until additional design cycles have been completed (see below).
	• An initial draft of the content development plan can be prepared, indicating who will be responsible and giving an estimate of how much material will be needed.
	• Content writing, media development, and programming can now be estimated for the overall project plan.
	• The biggest planning risk lies with objectives for which no solutions have yet been prototyped.
Additional Design	• Except for small projects and those with a very narrow focus, there won't be enough time to create final prototypes for all behavioral objectives.
	• Additional prototypes can be created with a smaller team and, if necessary, even without some of the key people, although their participation is always to be preferred.
	• The same iterative process of design—prototype— review is used. The key decision-makers should approve the additional prototypes before development commences.

Iterative Development	**Develop so that stakeholders continue to have a means of evaluating decisions and making corrections within project constraints.**
Develop—Implement—Evaluate	• The same fundamental concept of taking small steps, providing the work for review, and checking with key stakeholders, continues in development.
	• In contrast to the Iterative Design phase, each successive development cycle is a named iteration of the process and has a specific output product.
	• Note the arrow pointed from iterative development backward to iterative design. Sometimes an idea comes up in development that seems more economical, easier to develop, or just plain better. Rather than toss a coin or just chance it, the idea is thrown back for some quick prototyping and evaluation.
Cycle 1: Construction Cycle	• Prototypes serve as general development blueprints, but there are many details yet to be sorted out in the first development cycle—the Construction Cycle.
	• This cycle provides a time to confirm all design decisions made by actually presenting and testing a functional application on the intended delivery platform. The application is called a Design Proof.
Product: Design Proof	• Design Proofs combine sample content, including examples of all components, even if not all are integrated. The text and media included are polished and representative of the final quality to be expected for all similar elements.
	• Design Proofs are used to scout out potential problems so they don't become last-minute issues.

Cycle 2: Production Cycle	• The Production Cycle is focused almost entirely on developing approved designs. Production models (reusable software structures) are built where applicable. Full content development and integration occurs. The major outcome of the production phase is the Alpha Release.
Product: Alpha Release	• The Alpha Release is nearly the final version of the complete instructional application to be validated against the approved design. All content and media are implemented. Bugs are few, minor, and documented; none prevent learners from working through the full application.
	• Evaluation of the Alpha Release is expected to find few deviations from style guides, and only minor writing issues, graphical errors, and functional problems.
Cycle 3: Validation Cycle	• During the Validation Cycle, the Alpha Release is modified to reflect changes identified in its evaluation review. The resulting Beta Release is viewed as a first Gold Release candidate. There should be no functional errors at this stage.
Product: Beta Release	• The Beta Release is implemented on the final platform for dissemination, if this has not been done previously.
Correction Cycle(s)	• If problems are identified, they must be rectified before the Beta Release can be given the gold crown. A modified version of a Beta becomes Gold Candidate 2, and, if necessary, a succession of candidates are numbered until all problems are resolved.
Product: Gold Release	• When the Beta Release performs as expected and no additional problems are identified, it becomes the Gold Release and is ready for its final evaluations, such as determining whether identified behaviors are actually exhibited by the target audience and whether these new behaviors achieve the organizational success expected.

and frequency. While the iterative design cycles are taken very fast, over a period of a few days or less, iterative development cycles may take much longer. This corresponds to the increasing certainty with which team members know what they want and are less and less likely to be making fundamental mistakes or missing precious opportunities.

The previous table itemizes each of the phases and their functions, including descriptions of the specific activities that occur within each phase.

A note on quality assurance

In many ways, successive approximation instantiates the principles that experts in quality assurance espouse most strongly. Chief among them is the notion that quality is best attained by planning for it at the beginning of the process and assuring its attainment throughout, rather than only near the end of product production.

There is, therefore, no single event marked "Quality Assurance" in the diagram. Rather, quality assessment is done both within each segment of work and, most notably, at the end of each cycle of design and development in the repeated reviews and

evaluations. It remains important to establish criteria ahead of time and measure achievements against those criteria.

As an administrative matter, your team should submit for review and approval the set of criteria you propose to use for quality assurance in each phase of the process. You might do this in the form of evaluation checklists. Sample evaluation checklists that can help you get started on developing your own are provided for each developmental release in Chapter 15. You will also want to submit style guides for approval. Be sure to adapt general style guides you use, if any, for consistency with the rapid prototypes that served as the basis for your project plan.

During the design and development process, you will be checking on the following quality attributes of the work in progress:

Appropriateness

Does the application meet the learner needs as identified in the Project Plan and the Savvy Start?

Resource

Download checklists from: www. alleni.com/books/checklists.htm

Are language and media suitable and proper for the audience, culture, and values of the organization?

Correctness

Are media elements accurate and placed properly? Is all text spelled correctly? Is grammar correct?

Functionality

Do all links, navigation, animations, and learner response evaluations work properly? Are performance data captured correctly? Do sessions terminate properly, and are bookmarks functional?

Usability

Are interactions and controls intuitive and free from ambiguity? Are perceived effort and response time commensurate with the value of each operation? Are all "destructive" events safeguarded from accidental use and are recovery mechanisms available?

Design Consistency

Do all elements adhere to client and team approved design requirements? Are terms, icons, and controls used and placed consistently throughout?

Psychological Impact

Perhaps most often overlooked is how people feel when they use a learning application, but if the application makes learners uncomfortable and/or unhappy, it's doubtful the learning experience will be successful. Do users feel victimized? Do they feel burdened and bogged down, or do they feel energized and empowered?

9 | Preparing for a Savvy Start

1. Purpose of the Savvy Start
2. Criteria for a Successful Savvy Start
3. Agenda
4. Rules of Conduct
5. Backgrounding Information
6. Samples of e-Learning

Be Prepared

Successive approximation moves right into iterative design activities after backgrounding has collected useful information about needs and, most importantly, determined who should be involved in the initial, decision-making activities called the Savvy Start. The Savvy Start is essentially a group review of background information and the first, critical, rapid prototyping sessions that set the direction for the entire project.

It's hard to assemble a diverse group of the organization's key people and get any appreciable amount of their time together. Hoping to do so on a repeated or continuing basis is usually unrealis-tic. It's for this reason that successive approximation uses a carefully structured kickoff event.

By participating for only a very short amount of time, key people can become involved enough to both own and direct the project and assure everyone that it's on good footing. Within a period of two or three days, major design decisions are made, goals are reaffirmed, and primary assumptions are tested.

If the project is either a small one or one that will center on a small number of interactive designs, it may not be necessary to have further rapid prototyping cycles. In many cases, however, the Savvy Start accomplishes just the initial, but critical tasks with respect to achieving consensus among key stakeholders, establishing priorities, making sure that e-learning (whether blended or otherwise) is an appropriate solution, and fitting the design to the learner population. After a project plan is written, based on the work done in the Savvy Start, additional design prototyping is usually necessary.

The savvy team

I stressed identification of the right players in earlier chapters because it's so important to have the right people participate in the Savvy Start. This is really your first major challenge, in part because the right people don't often know who they are. In fact, the right people are sometimes pretty sure they aren't the right people, and you need to convince them otherwise in order to get their participation.

Once again, here's the list:
➤ Budget maker
➤ Person who owns the performance problem
➤ Person who supervises the performance
➤ Someone who knows the content
➤ Candidate learners
➤ Recent learners
➤ Project manager
➤ You, of course—the event leader
➤ An instructional designer
➤ A prototyper

Even you might not think they're the right people, but I hope I've already convinced you of their importance. If not, the proof is, well, in the meeting. Feel free to experiment. You might find you have better success with a slightly different group composition. It's rarely possible to fully get the prescribed mix, even though one insists (as I do).

If you were able to get the full complement of people to participate in the Savvy Start, and no one covered multiple roles, you'd have ten people. Ten people make a large group for the process. Although I've personally handled groups of over twenty, I wouldn't recommend it.

Smaller groups are usually easier to work with, but you'll have to come up with ways to make up for the loss that any absence inflicts. You really do need all these perspectives to guide you. You will usually find that one person can adequately represent more than one of these critical perspectives, providing the means for keeping the group smaller. For example, the budget maker may also own the performance problem. You might be able to lead the event and provide instructional design expertise. The organization's project manager might also supervise performers, and so on.

A private note

I have quite a sensitive issue to discuss with you here, and I'd rather you just kept it between us. No one from IT is on this list. Nor is there anyone from the legal department, HR, user interface, branding, or other standards bearers. We do need to keep in mind the devastating consequences of not inviting everyone to the party when Sleeping Beauty was born—a 100-year sleep and more. Sometimes, not inviting someone guarantees his or her opposition, or at least a lack of support.

A successful e-learning project really needs IT's support and compliance with many standards. It would therefore seem to be a good idea to invite all those who represent concerns to the project launch.

Neglecting to invite them because the group would be too large seems all too similar to the flimsy excuse Sleeping Beauty's father, the king, had when he explained that he had only twelve golden plates and therefore only twelve could come. The problems a lack of IT support, for example, can inflict on a potentially successful e-learning project are formidable.

But, and there's a big but, experience teaches those who have done many Savvy Starts that this isn't typically a productive venue for these personnel. They tend to focus on issues that can stifle the search for creative solutions. While their issues may be very important, it's equally important to explore first what solutions would be effective. Achieving the performance necessary for an organization to succeed is truly a critical mission and enough of a challenge for the initial exercise.

In the Savvy Start, we seek to find what solutions could work and what would be necessary to deliver them. Once we know that, we can look at whether current systems are sufficient, whether outsourced delivery would be necessary and viable, or whether the behavioral performance achievable is worth the cost. We can look at legal issues, wording standards, logo positioning, image and brand compatibility, and so on, once we know where our degrees of freedom lie and what our true necessities are.

It can be helpful, of course, to be prepared with information that could limit the range of viable solutions for the current organization. The risk is that you will only consider the convenient options, as opposed to those that would truly succeed but warrant and incur departure from previous restrictions and venturing into new paths, not to mention the costs.

Change is hard for most organizations, and difficult solutions aren't necessarily better than easy ones. So try to know all you can about what's easy and what's difficult for your organization. Get answers to the questions in the Technical Preferences for e-Learning Delivery (see the check list on the following page). If you handle this right, IT will appreciate your consulting with them and asking these questions. And they might very much appreciate not having to go to another meeting.

Preparing for the meeting

The Savvy Start is an intense two or three days, consuming some very valuable time, given the level of people you're going to have there. They will expect the meeting to be constructive. And because some of them probably had doubts that their participation was really warranted, you'll need to demonstrate their value to the process as soon as possible. To do all this, you'll need to be prepared.

Preparing discussion material

You will need to have at least the following materials ready to present:

1. Purpose of the Savvy Start

Be ready to express in your own words the purpose of the Savvy Start, which is to get a new learning initiative launched in the most expedient and successful way. The challenge to the group is to set project goals, provide ongoing support, make essential resources available, and establish a measurement of success.

Technical Preferences for e-Learning Delivery

Delivery parameters

1. Will this project be delivered on CD-ROM?
   - ❏ Yes. If Yes, see the section about CD-ROM delivery.
   - ❏ No
   - ❏ Both Web delivery and CD-ROM delivery

2. Is this a standalone solution, delivered with an executable?
   - ❏ Yes. If Yes, see question 3.
   - ❏ No. If No, this is a browser solution; see the browser section.

3. What versions of the standalone application do we need?
   - ❏ Mac _____
   - ❏ Windows _____
   - ❏ Unix _____

4. Is there tracking associated with this course?
   - ❏ Yes. If Yes, see the Tracking section.
   - ❏ No.

Browser

1. Which browsers need to be supported?
   - ❏ Mac _____
     - ○ Internet Explorer versions:_____
     - ○ Safari versions:_____
     - ○ Mozilla versions:_____
     - ○ Netscape versions:____
     - ○ Firefox versions:_____
   - ❏ Linux _____
     - ○ Internet Explorer versions:_____
     - ○ Mozilla versions:_____
     - ○ Netscape versions:____
     - ○ Firefox versions:_____
   - ❏ Windows _____
     - ○ Internet Explorer versions:_____
     - ○ Mozilla versions:_____
     - ○ Netscape versions:____
     - ○ Firefox versions:_____

2. What is the connection speed?
   - ❑ Analog Modem – Min. Speed 33.6DSL
   - ❑ Cable Modem
   - ❑ T1
   - ❑ LAN
   - ❑ Bandwidth Available:_____

3. Does the e-learning software need to detect versions of the Flash plugin?
   - ❑ Yes
   - ❑ No

4. Do the users have the ability to download the Flash plugin?
   - ❑ Yes
   - ❑ No

5. What version of the Flash plugin will be supported?

Tracking and LMS solution

1. What data should be tracked?
   - ❑ Completion
     - ○ Completion with no scoring
     - ○ Of lesson or module
   - OR
   - ❑ Pass / Fail
   - ❑ Time
     - ○ Entire course
     - ○ Lesson or module
     - ○ Other _____
   - ❑ Pre-score
   - ❑ Post-score
   - ❑ Bookmarking (current status)
   - ❑ Other _____

2. How should data be tracked?
   - ❑ LMS (JavaScript 2.0 will be required)
     - ○ Is it AICC compliant?
       - ○ Yes. If Yes, the impact to reporting is:
       - ○ No

○ SCORM compliant?
    ○ Yes. If Yes, the impact to reporting is:
    ○ No
○ Any other compliancy requirements?
    ○ Yes
    ○ No
○ None of the above
○ Is this a cross-domain solution?
    ○ Yes
    ○ No

❑ SharedObjects (Flash 6.0 and higher)
❑ Cookies (JavaScript required)
❑ Database. What kind of database is it? Please describe.

3. Is a custom tracking solution required?
    ❑ Yes. System is in place.
    ❑ Yes. System is being developed by others.
    ❑ Yes. System must be developed as part of the project
    ❑ No

CD-ROM delivery

1. Is artwork needed for the CD label?
    ❑ Yes
    ❑ No

2. Do we need to create an installation routine?
    ❑ Yes
    ❑ No

3. Who will duplicate CDs?

4. Does the program need to auto-run from the CD?
    ❑ Yes
    ❑ No

5. Is a custom icon needed for the installation routine?
    ❑ Yes
    ❑ No

Media

1. What should be the screen resolution?
   - ❏ 640 x 480
   - ❏ 800 x 600
   - ❏ 1024 x 768
   - ❏ _____

2. Multimedia requirements:
   - ❏ Audio – Narration
   - ❏ Audio – Sound Effects
   - ❏ Audio – Music
   - ❏ Video

3. Must the application scale to a resizable window?
   - ❏ Yes
   - ❏ No

4. What are the minimum processor and RAM requirements? _____

The Savvy Start will also determine in some detail the primary characteristics of the design, including its primary approach (such as game, simulation, scenario-based practice, etc.), its implementation (such as blended, independent, synchronous, asynchronous, Web, etc.), and the post-training support learners will be given. The group will develop at least a few rough prototypes of designs that everyone agrees have a strong probability of succeeding.

2. Criteria for a successful Savvy Start

Although the order of events and addressing issues will vary depending on the group's experience, preferences, and comfort, the Savvy Start will be successful only if:

➤ The targeted behavioral change is a change that addresses an organizational priority and is a realistic change.

➤ The targeted behavioral change is a change that can be facilitated by learning.

➤ Several design prototypes are developed and *discarded*. (Yes, discarded! To make the most of the process and to be assured you've found the best solution workable within project constraints, it's important to make the smallest possible investment in each prototype so that discarding it in favor of something better will be a no-brainer.)

➤ The group agrees that one or more prototypes represent learning experiences that are likely to be meaningful, memorable, and motivational for the targeted learning group and will develop behavioral skills that will be instrumental in meeting the organization's goal.

3. Agenda

Know the agenda. Have it neatly prepared, both in hardcopy and electronic slides. (See the sample agenda on pages 94-98.) Note timeframes, but be flexible as long as you are achieving the purpose of the Savvy Start. You want to use everyone's time to greatest advantage and keep everyone engaged throughout a fairly long, concentrated effort.

Check to see whether there will be unavoidable interruptions. If so, see if they can be scheduled so that everyone takes breaks together. There are times that you need to work privately with your prototyper.

These are good times for others to handle responsibilities that can't be postponed. The problem will be, of course, reeling them back in after they've gone off.

4. Rules of conduct

Successful Savvy Starts are almost always very enjoyable experiences. They are quite often punctuated with laughter, fascinating anecdotes, and the unique satisfaction that comes with the arrival of great ideas and insights. At the conclusion of a Savvy Start, participants nearly always comment with much enthusiasm that it was a great experience that produced outcomes they could not have achieved any other way.

Much of the work in Savvy Starts is brainstorming. It builds on the unique knowledge and experience of the people assembled. If the team is well-comprised, there will not be much redundancy. In any case, everyone's ideas and opinions are of value and appreciated. Differences of opinion often reveal information that becomes important to the project's success.

Therefore, a key rule is that no one belittles or even evaluates expressed ideas as they're being thrown out. There will be a time for idea evaluation. The event leader will clearly identify such a time.

It helps to conduct this meeting away from the organization's offices or place of business. Otherwise, it seems that people are called out at exactly the wrong times, discussions lose momentum, and things go off track. Everyone wonders what might have happened, had the interruption not occurred. There's a feeling that something valuable was lost forever.

The group really needs to be sequestered, to the extent possible, so that what otherwise typically takes weeks to accomplish, the Savvy Start can accomplish in only a few days.

Perhaps needless to say, but I think it's important, the rules must include a no-cell-phone policy. If necessary, phones can be used at breaks. Even this should be minimized, as discussions at breaks often produce some of the most creative or helpful ideas.

5. Backgrounding information

Your research will have uncovered important information for you to relay to the group. You should have this information organized and ready for distribution. You should also have it on electronic slides to help you talk through it.

Some of the standard things to include are:

> Related current training, if any; strengths and weaknesses.

> Organizational responsibilities for training as you understand them.

> Goal information. (There are probably multiple points of view on what the goal is or should be. Multiple goals may all be achievable, but some or all of them may be incompatible with the others for any number of reasons. A discussion on this will be valuable. Expect the goal and the measures of project success to change somewhat, and be open to it changing completely.)

> Any known constraints, such as schedule, budget, and legal requirements. (You can hope they will change as necessary to support a good solution to the identified goal. Be ready to discuss reducing project scope if resources require it, and even be ready to suggest abandoning e-learning completely if it becomes clear it's not a fitting solution.)

6. Samples of e-learning, good and bad

The differences between boring e-learning and effective on-target e-learning are huge, but it can be hard for people who haven't witnessed really good e-learning to recognize them. You want the discussion to focus on learning events that can change behavioral skills, but those unfamiliar with great e-learning will naturally tend to focus on content.

Examples of good e-learning really help give people ideas that they wouldn't otherwise have. Examples of poor e-learning, especially poor e-learning that looks good but doesn't engage learners, especially help participants frame for themselves what they want to achieve and avoid.

You have at the point of preparing for the Savvy Start, I hope, the answers to the Top Ten background questions (See pages 46-47). The answers to the goal and context questions are the information you'll want to present early in the meeting. You may have obtained different answers from every person. That's common. Don't let it bother you at this point. You'll be working to bring people to consensus in an efficient way. But you need to be sure you're aware of the different perspectives and can present them clearly without having to identify who expressed them to you. Remember, you're going to have people who rank at very different points on the organizational totem pole. The highest-ranking person won't necessarily have the keenest insight into the real problem, but lower-ranking persons may have difficulty expressing their views in this context. You'll do it for them.

Preparing the meeting room

You'll want a room that comfortably accommodates the number of people you have, of course, but you'll also want some pacing room. You'll be working together over quite a few hours, and it helps many of us to think and keep alert if we can stand and move around a bit without calling the meeting into recess.

Be sure there's a projector that's compatible with your computer and the one your prototyper will use. It's really handy to have two projectors. There will be many uses for them. You might, for example, want to have the good and poor e-learning examples up at the same time for comparison, or you might want to

have one screen to list reactions to a prototype that's on the other screen. Looking at two prototypes side by side can be very constructive.

You'll also make use of flip charts and markers. Have tape and/or thumbtacks handy if your flip-chart paper doesn't have adhesive.

Although it's common for the prototyper to do some work on a laptop while listening to your discussions and also at night between meetings, sometimes it's helpful to have a separate room nearby. The prototyper can move to that room for some concentrated work to build something faster.

Preparing for fun

Because you want the end product to energize and engage learners, you'll most often want to develop a fun learning experience. It helps if your team is having fun and thinking *fun* as they work, so it's smart to create a fun atmosphere right from the start.

You might bring some fascinating toys for early arrivals to play with. At the appropriate time you can ask the group what makes the toys so interesting. Why do we want to play with them? What makes them fun? The answers may yield some characteristics you want to work into your design.

You might dress your team in a fun uniform. Matching T-shirts with a well-chosen message could do the trick. At one Savvy Start, the members from one of our studios arrived in bright orange overalls, ready to *overhaul* the organization's training.

Just a small effort can make the difference between another laborious meeting and a creative, energetic collaboration that produces a meaningful, memorable, and motivational learning experience.

Think What could be done at the outset of a Savvy Start to put participants in both a fun and constructive mood?

Savvy Start Agenda

Savvy Start Day 1

1 hour	**1.1 Kickoff**

1.1 Introduction of attendees.

1.2 Discuss prototyping process and review the agenda for the next three days.

1.3 Review e-learning possibilities; demonstrate differences between good and poor e-learning.

1 hour	**2.0 Discuss Learning Goals for Project**

2.1 Discuss organization's desired performance goals in behavioral terms.

2.2 Present the training/learning climate and readiness for technology-supported learning as understood from backgrounding.

2.3 Review the criteria for success: How will we measure the learners' success?

2.4 Review previous work done.

2.5 Listen to a recent learner's story and solicit the supervisor's and SME's input.

2.6 Create a strategic map of what the instruction should accomplish.

1 hour	**3.0 Brainstorm Prototype 1**

3.1 Review the objectives and discuss the goals of topic to prototype. What do learners really need to do?

3.2 Discuss how to determine what needs to be taught.

3.3 Discuss the necessity of the learner's motivation to learn. What design elements can be used to heighten motivation?

3.4 Brainstorm learning events.

1 and 1/2 hours (working through lunch break)	**4.0 Build Prototype 1** 4.1 Designer and prototyper brainstorm further approaches and build an interaction. 4.2 Everyone else is free to check email, go back to work, etc. 4.3 Summon the team.
45 minutes	**5.0 Review Prototype 1 and Discuss Next Steps** 5.1 Team comes to review the prototype created. 5.2 Discuss improvements, possibly brainstorm further approaches, etc. What worked? What didn't? 5.3 Plan next steps. Debrief the prototyping process. What happens next? Who else gets involved? How do we move forward?
45 minutes	**6.0 Brainstorm Prototype 2** (different content)
1 hours	**7.0 Build Prototype 2** (different content)

Savvy Start Day 2

1/2 hour	**8.0 Review Prototype 2**
1/2 hour	**9.0 User Feedback** 9.1 Discuss importance of user feedback at this point. 9.2 Discuss logistics of obtaining learner feedback
1/2 hour – 45 minutes	**10.0 Delivery Platform, Assessment, and Tracking** 10.1 Discuss delivery platform capabilities and restrictions. 10.2 Review goals for assessment. 10.3 Stipulate assessments. 10.4 Discuss performance tracking mechanisms (e.g., logging in) and issues. 10.5 Determine compliancy issues (if any). 10.6 Review the role of formal instructional objectives.

1/2 hour	**11.0 Write Objectives**

11.1 Review the organization's goal; restate if appropriate.

11.2 Write one or two objectives.

11.3 Discuss resources and responsibilities. Who is going to analyze behaviors the Savvy Start team won't address and write corresponding objectives? How will consensus be achieved for these additional course objectives?

45 minutes	**12.0 Brainstorm Prototype 3** (new content)

lunch break

2 hours	**13.0 Build Prototype 3**
1/2 hour	**14.0 Review Prototype 3**
1/2 hour	**15.0 Brainstorm Prototype 4** (New content or build off an existing prototype, depending on what's needed.)
1 and 1/2 hours	**16.0 Build Prototype 4**
1/2 hour	**17.0 Review Prototype 4**

Savvy Start Day 3

15 minutes	**18.0 Prototypes in Context**

18.1 Review the process for creating the complete application (completion of Objectives x Treatments Matrix, integrating prototypes, number of cycles needed, integrating media, and developing the alpha, beta, and gold versions).

18.2 Discuss need for and means of gathering user feedback.

1 hour	**19.0 The Perfect Solution**

19.1 Describe the perfect solution, given your conversations throughout the previous two days regarding need, analysis, gap, potential solutions, tracking, assessments, etc.:

- What items would it track?
- How would you know learners gained knowledge and experience?
- What kind of reporting data would it generate?
- How would it be accessed, and what type of security would be present?

19.2 As you think about the ideal solution, discuss who is best prepared to contribute to it. Who, for example, can contribute not only content expertise, but also learning and performance inspiration?

1/2 hour	**20.0 Project Constraints**
	20.1 Budget and timeline
	20.2 SME access and content
	20.3 Project teams, approvals, decision-making
1/2 hour	**21.0 Media**
	21.1 Present a variety of applications using different approaches to media. Discuss pros and cons of different styles.
	21.2 Gather feedback and opinions on what defines the desired look and feel.
	21.3 Discuss sound, video, animation . . . anything that can impact performance of running WBT.
45 minutes	**22.0 Brainstorm Prototype 5**
	22.1 New content or build off an existing prototype? Depends on what's needed.
	22.2 Integrate anything that comes up during the "comprehensive solution" approach.
lunch break	
1 and 1/2 hours	**23.0 Build Prototype 5**
1/2 hour	**24.0 Review Prototype 5**

45 minutes

25.0 Final Strategy Review

25.1 Review project risks.

25.2 Discuss what to expect in the project plan.

25.3 Discuss any final questions about next steps, the process as a whole.

10 | Project Kickoff

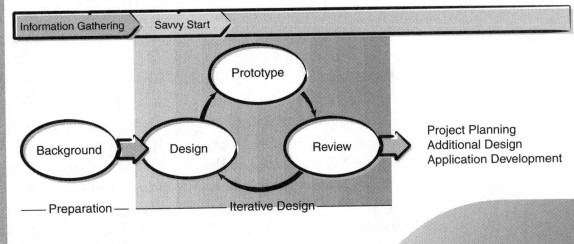

Spinning into control

Day 1 of your three-day Savvy Start has arrived. With persistence and a convincing message, you've prevailed. The right team is showing up and you're taking the leap. The process is clear in mind, as is the simple visual you'll be putting up (see figure above).

Conducting the meeting

It's important for you to establish your leadership and set ground rules. The rules need not be stated in a dictatorial manner, of course; but you do want the group to lend you authority if you are going to take the responsibility of a successful event.

You might say something like this:

"We have a great opportunity before us. Your time is precious, and it's important for us to use our time very productively. There are many fascinating things we could talk about, because e-learning is rich with opportunities, so we'll have to work hard to remain focused on the right things. I do want to make sure that everyone's ideas are voiced and concerns are taken into account.

"Therefore, I'm going to brazenly ask for

Яapid reader

- The Savvy Start kicks off the project by reviewing needs and reconfirming goals.

- A demonstration of successful and unsuccessful e-learning applications helps everyone focus on key issues.

- Success criteria and a strategic map are established.

your permission to direct the discussion. I'll need to cut off discussions sometimes, introduce new topics abruptly, and otherwise determine what's productive and what should wait for another time or venue.

"Is everyone ok with this?"

You'll have to work out your own response if someone objects. That very rarely happens at first. It will happen later, however, if people don't feel the meeting is productive. You have a lot to accomplish, so you shouldn't have trouble if you can keep things moving. Your biggest risk is the dominating talker—someone who drones on and on about his or her experiences or theories of learning.

The other potential major problem you'll have is subordinated thinking—that is, people not expressing their true thoughts by either saying nothing or saying only things that support the expressed or known thoughts of others higher in the organization's hierarchy.

The 1-minute trick

Here's a tip that helps control both talkers and subordinated thinkers. Ask everyone in succession for an idea or opinion that hasn't yet been expressed.

Everyone has to say something. It just has to be different, but it doesn't need to be a thought that even its contributor agrees with. Stupid, off-the-wall responses help keep things lighthearted and can help others offer contradictory opinions in a euphemistic tone to camouflage their serious feelings. It's all ok if it puts important thoughts and concerns on the table.

And here's the trick: Use a timer or your watch to give people only 1 minute to come up with and express each thought—maybe only 30 seconds.

Because of the time constraint, people scramble to say anything that gets them through their minute. Sometimes, just to get off the hook, people will throw out the opposite of what someone else just said. There's a laugh, no offense, and a discussion item that might not have come out is now listed.

If you feel there are still unexpressed concerns, or should be, keep the process going. You can do this until no one feels he or she can say anything meaningful. Don't forget to include yourself and your team in this as well.

Present the agenda

Let's take a close look at the agenda. We'll look at a typical three-day Savvy Start. Refer back to page 94 for a complete sample agenda.

It will be smart to spend a little time reviewing the agenda with the group, as it will help you re-state and explain the process as well as just set forth the schedule. Of course, if your team has recently completed one or more Savvy Starts, you'll be able to skip through this quickly.

1.1 Introduction of attendees

You'll want to set a friendly, collaborative tone for the event immediately. You can do this many ways, so be sure to choose an approach that's comfortable for you. Having your team there in bright red overalls can work beautifully if you have the confidence and sense of humor needed to pull it off.

Unless you know for sure, you shouldn't assume people know each other—especially in large organizations. We really want to minimize the stifling effects of aristocratic posturing. Although you can't prevent people from stating their titles, you can try. There are many techniques.

Try this. When you go around the room asking people to introduce themselves, say, "Everyone's opinion is vital to our collective success. If others could contribute what your position uniquely prepares you to say, you wouldn't be here.

"As we go around the room to make quick introductions, it would be great if you'd just give us your name, a description of one of your most memorable learning events, and what you hope we'll achieve through the development of this learning solution."

1.2 Discuss prototyping process and review the agenda

Note for the team that the process is essentially one of brainstorming and experimentation made practical: "While we think we understand the primary mission, we must be open to the discovery that we might find bigger, better, or more useful things that can be done. We should be looking for the low-cost opportunities to do great things, and because of the successive approximation process being used, we might just find them in places we aren't really looking."

> **1.0 Kickoff** ◁

1.1 Introduction of attendees.

1.2 Discuss prototyping process and review the agenda for the next three days.

1.3 Review e-learning possibilities; demonstrate differences between good and poor e-learning.

1.3 Review e-learning possibilities

The best e-learning is **m**eaningful, **m**emorable, and **m**otivational. It generates **m**easurable results (the 3 Ms + 1). You can talk about these

---

Resource

⌨ www.alleni.com/books/demos. htm for demos of the 3Ms in action

---

attributes, how easy it is to produce boring e-learning that's essentially worthless, and how much more important it is to focus on outcome behaviors than on "content that our people must know." But until people actually witness the differences between the kinds of e-learning that really work and the unfortunately typical e-learning that simply throws content at learners (with a posttest at the end), they have trouble really understanding the difference.

So here's where you'll demonstrate both good and poor e-learning, and also either demonstrate or describe various blended structures that are valuable in different situations.

2.1 Discuss organization's desired performance goals

If this is a business problem you're addressing, you should speak in standard business terms and use concepts specific to the business's operations. You might address such things as margins, return on investment, productivity, mean time to market, process throughput, and so on. In specific fields, bone up, if you need to, on primary terms so you can use them comfortably. Speak knowledgeably of reciprocity failure, aero modular technology, adhesive capsulitis, mulligatawny soup, six sigma analysis, or whatever is directly germane to the organization's performance concern.

Most important: Remember that the goal is not training. Training is a means to an achievement that is important to the organization. It's very easy to get on the wrong track if the group loses this perspective.

You will want agreement on what behavioral changes are necessary to accomplish the organization's goal. To make sure that the behavioral changes are not divorced from the

> **▷ 2.0 Discuss learning goals ◁**

2.1 Discuss organization's desired performance goals in behavioral terms.

2.2 Present the training/learning climate and readiness for technology-supported learning as understood from backgrounding.

2.3 Review the criteria for success: How will we measure the learners' success?

2.4 Review previous work done.

2.5 Listen to a recent learner's story and solicit the supervisor's and SME's input.

2.6 Create a strategic map of what the instruction should accomplish.

primary justification for making them, try working backwards. At the top of a flip chart, write the primary goal. Under that, make two columns. In the left column, write the current behavior that contributes to the problem. In the right column, describe the behaviors that would alleviate the problem.

This simple exercise is a great way to keep the functional perspective you need. Once this page is filled out and taped on the wall, you'll find it helpful to refer to it often—especially when you sense discussions are getting off track.

Keep your eye on the primary goal. It may need to be restated as you work. Sometimes, as groups list the behaviors they want, they realize some behaviors don't have much to do with the primary goal as stated. If the unrelated behaviors are of paramount importance, it's useful to find out why. The group may have discovered there's a more comprehensive or important goal to pursue.

2.2 Present the training/learning climate

Often unrecognized are attributes of the learning environment that can inhibit successful instructional initiatives.

➤ Do learners value learning?

➤ Have previous instructional programs been boring time wasters?

➤ Do learners have computer access?

➤ Are computers located where learners can concentrate and work with sufficient privacy?

➤ Is there sufficient bandwidth and IT support? Are firewalls going to prevent use of needed communications and technology?

Our goal: Reduce by 20% product returns caused by missing parts. This problem costs us $1.5 million each year	
Problem behaviors	Desired behaviors

The climate doesn't need to be perfect, but there has to be hope that existing problems can be overcome. Your discussion will help you rule out certain solutions that would require too many organizational accommodations.

2.3 Review the criteria for success

This exercise hits on multiple fronts and helps confirm assumptions you are beginning to make, such as who is really in charge and what's truly the organization's goal. Make sure it's established how the primary decision-maker is going to know whether the project was a success or not.

Don't be tempted to accept the typical criteria—a project that runs smoothly, completes on time and within budget, includes all the prerequisite content, rolls out easily, and generates few learner complaints. While this is a tall order, indeed, and all these tasks must be accomplished, these aren't the criteria of success unless you've let the group lose their focus on the real goal.

Whether it's improved customer service, increased sales, reduced recalls, shorter time to market, reduced errors, better placement in graduate schools, or higher initial employment salaries, you need to establish how the impact of learning will be measured. Although at some point before the final project plan is approved, specific quantitative goals should be put in place, it's not necessary to do this now. Your meeting time will be depleted rapidly on all the things you need to accomplish, and a discussion of the exact numbers to target could become lengthy due to the consideration it deserves. But it's important that you establish at least the type of measures at this

point before designing the means to accomplish the goal.

2.4 Review previous work done

You don't want to repeat approaches that haven't worked, and you'll want to put in place a well-rounded solution that involves not only learning but also, for example, transition support and incentives. It's helpful to know what attempts have been made, such as changed incentives, modified processes, programs to hire more qualified people, additions of field trips, or use of mentors.

Either from background information you've gathered or from what the group can recount, review what's been tried, what the outcomes were, and what lessons have been learned.

2.5 Listen to a recent learner's story and solicit the supervisor's and SME's input

These three people are going to have a lot to offer if you've been able to get them to the Savvy Start. The recent learner's insights are often exceptionally helpful if you can make him or her comfortable enough to speak up. What was easy to learn? What was hard? Why was it hard, and what helped you "get" it? What did you find fascinating? What was boring? What have you found most useful? What was unnecessary?

The supervisor typically observes the successes and failures of people similar to those to be taught. Seek to learn what is difficult and easy, consequential and unimportant, frequently needed and seldom used.

SMEs vary in their ability to be helpful at this point. The paradox of expertise guides us here. The more knowledgeable people are, the more difficulty they have thinking as a novice and learner. What makes sense to them is often based on a perspective learners cannot take. SMEs sometimes also think good

instruction must cover everything they know, almost regardless of its utility and relationship to targeted behaviors.

You will ask the SME later to review the accuracy of content materials to be developed, and you'll also want the SME to inform you of any inaccuracies in existing materials you might use as a reference.

2.6 Create a strategic map of what the instruction should accomplish

Now, just before you begin brainstorming for the first prototypes, you can set forth a series of learning steps. You could think of this as a

Example of a Skills Hierarchy
Reproduced from *Michael Allen's Guide to e-Learning* with permission of the publisher

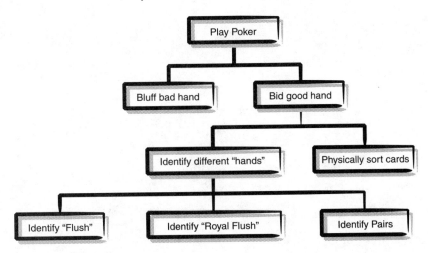

skills hierarchy, which, once again, you should construct backwards.

Put a selected, important, outcome behavior at the top. Underneath and at the same level as each other, put the primary prerequisite skills needed to perform the outcome behavior at the top. Underneath each of them, list their prerequisites. Continue downward until you're listing skills that are so rudimentary you can safely assume nearly all learners would have them.

Now, looking at the current behaviors that are problematic and at the needed behaviors, map out what seems like a reasonable progression of skills development. Don't automatically start at the top of the

skills hierarchy and work upward. The most interesting skills are usually found at higher levels and the boring ones at the bottom. It's not an optimal design to start with the most boring content.

Again, we'll take up instructional design principles in a companion book, but using an interesting context is vital. Contexts that are usually most interesting are those in which a skill has obvious utility. So look up as high as you need to in the hierarchy until you can find a context that would be interesting to learners. You are now ready to set forth these contexts as a backdrop for brainstorming and prototyping learning events.

11 | Rapid Design, Prototyping, and Review

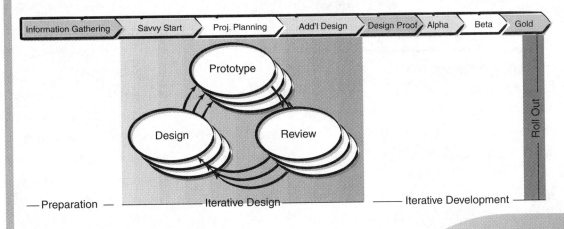

Information Gathering | Savvy Start | Proj. Planning | Add'l Design | Design Proof | Alpha | Beta | Gold

Prototype

Design

Review

Roll Out

— Preparation — | Iterative Design | Iterative Development

You've set the ground rules and focus for the creation of a learning solution. For many of us, and probably for you, you're ready for the most fun in the whole process. It's time to look at all the pieces of the challenge and find an exciting solution.

I must hasten to point out that you do not have to invent a new solution. Being original isn't really one of the criteria that needs to be met. Although it can be satisfying to devise a unique learning experience, you have enough challenges without adding any that are unnecessary. There are many excellent instructional paradigms you can use. The more you have seen, the more prepared you will be to suggest use of a design. Many professional designers have seen dozens if not hundreds of instructional designs. If you have an experienced designer on your team, you should expect him or her to recognize the applicability and inapplicability of designs as the group discusses various possibilities.

If you are familiar with many paradigms, be careful not to dominate the discussion or let anyone dictate what designs are and are not appropriate. There have been many

яapid reader

- Repeated cycles of rapid design, prototyping, and review occur within the Savvy Start.

- Viewing functional prototypes helps the team make major design decisions very quickly.

- Prototypes reduce varied expectations and miscommunications.

- Skilled prototypers are needed.

▷ 3.0 Brainstorm Prototype 1 ◁

3.1 Review the objectives and discuss the goals of topic to prototype. What do learners really need to do?

3.2 Discuss how to determine what needs to be taught.

3.3 Discuss the necessity of the learner's motivation to learn. What design elements can be used to heighten motivation?

3.4 Brainstorm learning events.

occasions on which I've felt pretty sure which paradigm would be best, yet by keeping quiet, listening, and working with the group, we came up with an unexpected twist, often to a model familiar to me, that moved from a design that would have been very good to a design that was great.

Rapid collaborative design

You may have to bite your tongue for a while. Nothing disables a team more than someone who repeatedly cites examples unknown to everyone else or makes a pretense of having the answers in advance of everyone else. So let the team put forward their ideas, regardless of whether they advance old ideas that have never worked or ones that wouldn't be appropriate in this case.

Not all groups brainstorm as effectively as others. You have the

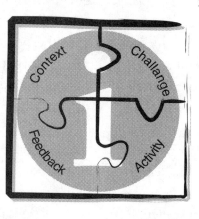

unusual mix of people and their disparate viewpoints working against you. The chemistry of the people, the place, and the time have a lot to do with its success, but so do you. You need to make everyone comfortable, ready to participate energetically, and able to overcome any creativity-inhibiting self-consciousness.

Tips for brainstorming

Let's go through the agenda for brainstorming; but remember, don't be overly structured or dictatorial here. Let things flow in a sequence that seems comfortable to the group.

3.1 What do learners really need to do?

This should all be fresh in everyone's minds and even up on the wall. You really want your team to think about behaviors learners need to be practicing toward the end of the e-learning. Think of this in terms of the four components that make up interactive learning events: context, challenge, activity, and feedback.

Context

You've already picked a point of interest on your skills hierarchy, so it should be easy to describe more contexts in which learners would need to perform those tasks. Some examples:

> ➤ On the phone with a person who ordered a winter parka and got three pairs of pink tights instead.
> ➤ Facing a customer who brought her car back because the radio doesn't work any better than when she brought it in for repair the first time.
> ➤ Dropping in on a restaurant owner who has decided to buy his cleaning supplies from one of your competitors.
> ➤ Needing to set up a medical device for a patient with heart arrhythmia.
> ➤ Updating online records for an insurance customer who has sold his car and bought a new one.

Choosing a robust context that's appealing to learners provides interest and the opportunity to practice authentic tasks. Get your group to propose several of them, then pick one to build on, being ready to reject it in favor of one of the others should you run into problems.

Challenges

See whether you can list multiple specific challenges that work in a single context. If you can, it will allow you some economies in development and might allow you to add realism-enhancing media to the context. For example, given the first context listed above:

> ➤ Challenge the learner to identify how most customers would like to have this situation resolved.
> ➤ Challenge the learner to identify some of the worst things a customer service agent could do in response to this situation.
> ➤ Challenge the learner to use the online system to place an order for the correct winter parka, send a postpaid mailer for returning the tights, and offer the customer a special discount on any additional item.

Activity

Move on to some examples of specific activities the learner could perform:

➤ In the context of a big lumberjack guy in pink tights angrily calling to complain, learners have 20 seconds after hearing his message to select the best thing one could say from a list of five messages.

➤ Using a simulated order-entry system, learners must recall the misprocessed order while also selecting a conversational message every 15 seconds that will keep the customer online and cooperative.

Feedback

Think about the kinds of feedback that would be effective. Usually most desirable is feedback that reveals the power of newly acquired skills. There are two elements to arrange:

1. Interactions that allow learners to perform multi-step tasks and require exactly the same decision-making skills and performance they will need in real life.
2. Intrinsic feedback; i.e., feedback that allows learners to witness the positive or negative consequences of their actions (as opposed to extrinsic feedback that simply tells learners whether they were right or wrong).

The order-processing example above yields great opportunities for multi-step tasks and intrinsic feedback. As learners select messages, callers can become increasingly understanding and cooperative, consistently annoyed but on the line, or increasingly angered to the point of hanging up or insistent on speaking to the learner's supervisor.

3.2 Discuss how to determine what needs to be taught

In order to create powerful learning experiences, it's almost always necessary to set aside some traditionally taught content, and even content that some of your team members may have a special affinity to. Thinking now from the perspective of the primary behavioral skills your team is trying to develop and the context in which you're going to have learners practicing these skills, it's easier to begin selecting essential content, identifying supportive and nice-to-know material, and weeding out the excess.

Promote the idea that the design needs only the content that helps learners develop and practice the skills you've identified in the context you've identified. Provide any concerned team members this comfort: Other content, if it's truly needed, will be required as you work later on other skills or other learning contexts. If, at the end of the process, you have content items that haven't been selected, it's likely that this is content that can and should be excluded. Or at least converted into a reference tool.

Hopefully, the team will accept your recommendation and avoid lengthy discussions about the utility of every potential content element. You want to keep the focus of discussions and brainstorming on the learning experiences and the learning they promote, not on content elements.

3.3 Discuss the necessity of the learner's motivation

The motivation learners actually have is usually different from what management or faculty hopes it is and/or perceives it to be. For example, faculty may assume students have enrolled in a psychology class to learn about the study of human behavior. Some probably did, but a number of students probably enrolled to avoid the alternative of biology or physics courses that, although they fulfill required science credits, are reputed to be much more difficult. These learners want a good grade in a course that fulfills a science requirement much more than they care about the study of human behavior. They will prepare themselves for graded activities, but not likely retain much of their knowledge of psychology past the end of the term.

Similarly, top management can easily think that employees are highly motivated to maximize corporate profits and provide top customer service as a means to that end, when many are actually motivated more to minimize risks of being criticized for errors or having to work extra hours.

Since learners must do their own learning (you cannot do it for them), they must have a minimum level of interest in learning. Otherwise, any instructional event will fail. Conversely with heightened motivation, almost any learning event is likely to have increased effectiveness. Successful designs therefore have a compelling attribute to them that holds learner attention from the beginning and throughout practice exercises that fully develop behavioral skills.

The Savvy Start team should consider motivational needs and

work to develop designs that would increase learner motivation.

3.4 Brainstorm learning events

The trick was to reach this point without exhausting the interest or energy of your team.
You may have had a lot to teach them.

Learning events are segments of instructional interactivity that hold together around a single context, as defined above. They can be a single point of interaction or a series of interactions.

The group will love brainstorming ideas for learning events, and it's time to do just that. If they got the messages you've worked hard to deliver and they understand the task before them reasonably well, you'll most likely experience fascinating progress in their brainstorming.

The objective, of course, is to list a bunch of different ideas. Some ideas will generate other ideas, often in a sequence of improving usefulness.

Step-by-step guide

You should improvise. No two Savvy Starts have ever been alike, and there are many reasons why each one should and will be unique. There's no substitute for using your good judgment; however, to give you a model you can visualize, here are the suggested steps:

Step 1. At first, list, write, or draw ideas rapidly. Get a sense of speed going. Try to be taping a new page to the wall from your flip chart every few minutes. A rapid-fire rhythm will help participants be more comfortable throwing out even their half-baked ideas. And that's what you want.

Ideas will come more slowly after a bit. It's ok to slow down after the initial blast (which might take a little time to start) and let people ponder a bit. Mostly likely, the later ideas will be combinations of things already suggested. If and when the discussion begins to move toward evaluation of ideas, stop the process for a moment.

Step 2. Ask the group to peruse the list, and ask, "What are we missing?" Discuss. List new ideas that come up.

Step 3. Check again, "Are we coming up with ideas that are engaging, authentic, and give learners the opportunity to build useful skills?" Discuss. List new ideas that come up.

Step 4. Then ask, "What are our best ideas?" Mark them, perhaps with a big circle just in front of them. You don't want more than two to five marked.

Step 5. Ask the group to rank the best ideas. Put a "1" in the circle by the best idea and number the other top ideas in their ranking order.

Step 6. Now, prepare two flip charts with clean sheets of paper. Put the name, title, or keyword of the number 1 idea at the top of both flip charts and underline it.

Step 7. On the first chart, make two columns, one for strengths and the other for weaknesses, and fill in the columns. Use the second chart to further define, describe, and visualize the design idea as you discuss it. Make the description as graphic as possible with rough sketches, arrows, and notes to clarify what things are and/or how they work.

As you do this, it's quite likely that a few new design ideas will pop up. You can add them to the brainstormed list, or, if it's really a modification of the number 1 idea that everyone endorses, just start again and make this idea number 1b.

Step 8. Once you've completed the definition, strengths, and weaknesses of a design idea, check to see whether your list of top ideas should be reordered. It's likely you've added an idea or two, and these might push some of your previous ideas down in ranking. Work through at least the next two top ideas in this same manner by repeating Steps 6 through 8.

Rapid prototyping

Prototypes are invaluable to the process and almost magic. They shorten the overall process time dramatically, improve information sharing among key stakeholders, and lead to more creative designs. Getting a product out faster is so important for many organizations that this benefit alone is enough to demand the use of rapid prototyping, but it's the additional capabilities of helping people talk more constructively and specifically about designs and of helping teams be more creative and effective in their design work that makes rapid prototyoing so extrodinarily valuable.

Prototypes vs. storyboards

For decades, designers have used storyboards. Each "page" of the application to be developed is sketched out on a separate piece of paper. Documentation describes how elements are to be developed, such as what the text will say and which media are to be placed where. It's a technique brought over from animated film making. I remember so clearly, as I imagine many people about my age do, when Walt Disney demonstrated on his weekly television program the use of storyboards he and his team used to create animated feature movies, such as *Snow White*. They taped pages and pages of sketches on the wall, replacing pages, rearranging them, and inserting more and more as they built on their initial ideas.

Rough sketches were eventually replaced with more detailed renderings, until they evolved into the final art. Voice recordings were made, and animation was added to match the sound track and transition from one key frame to another. It was a very effective process that has evolved today into the use of electronic storyboards through which roughly drawn art evolves into final renditions without ever going to paper.

The process of e-learning has, in some ways, followed the evolution of film animation, but e-learning gains an extra advantage by moving to the electronic medium: a way to experiment with interactivity.

Storyboards help the creators of movies concentrate on the sequence and flow of events, transition, and the overall effect they have on the audience. There will be only one sequence of events. All viewers will see the same movie. But with e-learning, we strive to make the sequence of events fit the individual. Designs that achieve the most often do so by providing experiences that are unique to the individual. To perfect these designs, we need *interactive* prototypes—not just paper-based storyboards that tend to focus more on the presentation of information than on conditional branching in response to learner behavior.

Beauty is in the eye of the beholder

Subtitle: Ugly is beautiful if you know what to look for.

The process is iterative because no matter what design item we might start with, it will have some dependency on items yet to be designed.

We generally want to begin with a statement of desired outcomes and envision what computer-based activities would cause a learner to be practicing nearly exactly those behaviors. Then determine what skills the learner would have to master just before being able to practice the target behaviors and figure out an interesting way for learners to acquire those skills. We would continue what's essentially the decomposition of each set of skills until we've reach an entry point.

To risk being a bit redundant, let me say again that it's not unusual during this process to realize the originally targeted outcome behaviors have been defined either too narrowly or two broadly. Sometimes groups discover that they have the wrong outcome behaviors entirely, but they simply didn't understand the performance context and challenges well enough to know that. Successive approximation often leads groups to insights they could not anticipate.

Realizing you need to change direction is an important step forward, and the process is there to continue guiding you to a good problem/solution definition. But, of course, you want to come to such realizations as quickly as possible. You want to invest as little time and energy as possible in your prototypes, because they may well be discarded.

The early prototypes should help groups get to the heart of the matter, and that heart is the context, challenge, activity, and feedback that provides the learning experience. It's not beautiful graphics, refined text, or a smooth navigation system. All these are important components of the final application, but at this early point, you want the group to focus on those design decisions that define the learning experiences to be refined.

Stick figures are really preferable, even if detailed photos or beautiful illustrations are available to drop in. It's unfortunate, perhaps, but use of refined media early on can actually obscure weaknesses in design. You really want the interactive components naked, so you can see as clearly as possible what you're doing. In the eye of the professional, an ugly screen is a beautiful thing at this point because it has wasted no time or effort and it exposes the design clearly.

Further, refined art (and even refined interactivity) sometimes

gather premature admiration. The Savvy team may become attached to a look or some bit of functionality that really should be abandoned in favor of designs that integrate and more fully support the final overall design. Refined elements can make a prototype look less fluid and less of an experiment. Teams can feel it would be wasteful or expensive to throw out refined elements, even if, in actuality, they were as inexpensive as clip art or a temporary reuse of previously developed elements. The unfortunate consequence is that team members may not suggest or even consider valuable changes.

On the other hand, some people have trouble seeing the difference between those things that are unimportant and easily changed and those that are critical and not easily changed once development gets underway. The graphic treatment is sometimes such a key component for those whose eye for interactivity isn't well developed, they cannot get

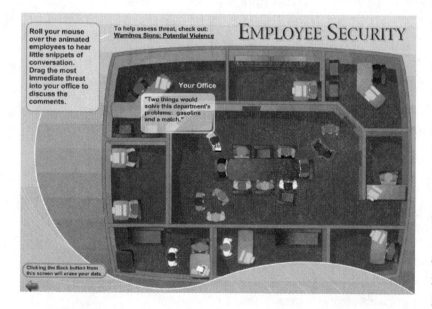

Ugly Prototypes Keep Focus on Primary Design Issues

Top: One aspect of critical decision-making came from this prototype. Bottom: The prototype also revealed need to compare warning signs and identify highest priority concerns in a typical office context as implemented in award-winning application shown here.

Resource

Download screen captures of prototypes and the final application designs to use as presentation aids from: www.alleni.com/books/prototypes.htm

a feel for the learning experience unless rough graphics are replaced with more refined ones.

Appreciating ugly

Most often you'll want to focus initially on creating prototypes that explore interactivity. Sometimes you can help newcomers develop an appreciation for quick-and-dirty visual components used in rapidly prototyping interactivity by showing them a final application that has a beautiful look to it and then showing them what the first prototypes looked like. The examples on these two pages show how rough initial prototypes evolved into refined applications.

If showing screen captures and explaining how rough prototypes help teams explore interactivity more quickly doesn't work, try creating multiple prototypes, each having a single purpose. This will help the team understand that dealing with too many issues at one time slows the process and introduces frustrating complexity.

Screen capture (left) courtesy of Corning, Inc. and (right) courtesy of Union Bank of California

Ugly Prototypes Keep Focus on Primary Design Issues

Top: This rough prototype explored ways learners could examine many checks to determine negotiability. Bottom: Realistic checks presented in the context of the current date made practice directly transferable to daily practice.

Consider these special-purpose prototypes:

> ➤ **A look and feel prototype** can deal with style; e.g. color, use of effects such as drop shadows, division of screen areas, use of mouse gestures, etc.

> ➤ **A media prototype** can explore use of sound effects, narration, 3D illustration, video, and so on.

> ➤ **A navigation prototype** can illustrate the capabilities to move from activity to activity, to access reference material and services such as glossary, notebook, and calculator, and to access personal performance data.

> ➤ **An interactivity prototype** can illustrate designs of the context, challenge, activity, and feedback that will define interactions.

For each of these prototypes, it's smart to spend minimal time on any components not being examined. Speed is of the essence, as you'll only have your group together for two or three days. You want to help the group focus most of their time on devising learning events. Although you can sometimes convince groups to simply set aside concerns about such things as navigation, media, or look and feel, if the group continues to be uneasy about details in those areas, they'll be able to dismiss them more easily if you first identify issues and preferences through special-purpose prototypes.

A good prototyper

Good prototypers are talented people indeed. They wield not only the essential technical skills to build functional prototypes quickly, but also listen carefully to discussions, isolate key factors, and, perhaps with the guidance of an instructional designer, concoct designs that both exemplify the strength of the group's ideas and apply sound principles of human learning.

A good prototyper:

> ➤ Keeps prototypes as simple as possible
> ➤ Avoids early media refinement
> ➤ Listens carefully and devises solutions that meet multiple criteria
> ➤ Works quickly
> ➤ Demonstrates options
> ➤ Makes contributions
> ➤ Has instructional design skills and a good sense of graphic design (even though not necessarily strong expertise in either)

➤ Is perfectly comfortable throwing prototypes away

➤ Is eager to explore alternatives

There's a paradox regarding who makes a good prototyper. Contrary to what you might expect, your best programmers and developers may not be your best prototypers. Prototypers need to suspend practices that are typically hallmarks of professional developers, such as carefully structuring code, naming all variables meaningfully, and organizing databases systematically. A good prototyper is fast, probably sloppy, and able to translate vague descriptions into prototypes that appear to be more functional than they are.

Good prototypers fake things and cheat, setting aside good development practices for speed. They are lazy in a way. They put the least amount of work possible into a prototype so they can get on to creating others. They aggressively search for shortcuts that save time and effort—shortcuts that would be shunned in the development of any work intended for use beyond a few hours.

Not all highly proficient developers can effectively abandon their usual professional scruples. Their sense of procedural propriety is too deeply ingrained. But some can and thereby churn out a whirlwind of useful prototypes. Prolific prototypers allow teams to make rapid design progress. And by exploring many alternatives in a short time, they steer the process toward the creative, fun, and effective e-learning everyone seeks.

Tips for Prototypers

➤ Suspend good programming practices that require time or thought; faster is better.

➤ Select targets that demonstrate ways e-learning stimulates thinking.

➤ Don't be concerned with media or a polished look.

➤ Fake everything you can.

➤ Limit combinatorial explosion (make options work only in predetermined sequences).

➤ Focus on interactivity (because people have trouble judging it until they can actually see it).

➤ Remember more prototypes are better than fewer, more complete prototypes.

Prototypers and their tools

The prototyper needs to be skilled in an authoring or a development tool to the point that he or she can make interactions functional in a very short amount of time. Authorware™ was designed from the ground up for this purpose, and many professionals use it for prototyping, as my studios do. But many other tools can be used if the developer has had enough experience to be quick about it.

Many people ask about using PowerPoint™ as a rapid prototyping tool. There are advantages to using it, not the least of which are its ubiquitous availability and the large number of people who have some skill with it. I don't advocate its usage for this purpose because it tends to be restrictive with respect to the interactivity most users can build or simulate. It also tends to put focus on content presentation rather than on the user's experience. But even with all these drawbacks, I have seen people use it very successfully for prototyping. If you have no better choice, then sure. But I would hope you might have better alternatives.

Working with prototypers

The prototyper will have been attending, and hopefully participating in, the Savvy Start discussions up to the point at which the group has completed the description of the design idea they consider to be their best. At this point, however, the prototyper may want to withdraw to another workspace in order to concentrate on developing a prototype of the idea as quickly as possible.

Many teams like to take a break at this point so the e-learning team can talk with the developer and suggest what should be done.

Your team is probably strongest if both a prototyper and an instructional designer assist you. These two individuals have the challenge of representing ideas agreed to by the team, and also the responsibility of shaping designs according to what experience and/or theory suggests would be the best way to implement the group's ideas. Prototypes should include not only a direct representation of the group's design ideas, as well as is possible, but also one or more alternatives. These alternatives would be hard for the group to appreciate through verbal description, but once they've seen their ideas implemented, they will be able to have meaningful discussions on permutations you think need consideration.

Building the first prototype

It's time for the group to experience the value of rapid prototypes. Sometimes your prototyper will actually have one ready for the group to review when their discussions come to a close. This happens when you have a talented prototyper who anticipates the group's conclusion and works with ears tuned toward their discussions while working quietly on one or more prototypes.

It's not unusual for this to happen, but you shouldn't count on it. At the last minute, the group's thinking may go off in an unanticipated direction, and it will be necessary to prototype a different solution. Here's how this typically works:

4.1 Designer and prototyper build an interaction

Although you may need to develop several special-purpose prototypes, as described above, your primary objective is to build key interactions that will serve as foundations for the development of the full application. It's often necessary for your designer and prototyper to take the ideas expressed by the group a bit further so that they become sufficiently specific and they are able to prototype them.

4.2 Group break

This is a good time for the group to take a break. They'll appreciate this, but you need to be sure you won't lose them. There's much work yet to do, but it will be somewhat difficult for you to know just how much time you'll need before the prototype is ready to review.

> **4.0 Build Prototype 1**
>
> 4.1 Designer and prototyper brainstorm approaches further and build an interaction.
>
> 4.2 Everyone else is free to check email, go back to work, etc.
>
> 4.3 Summon the team.

Make sure you have the means of getting in touch with everyone, and that they can reassemble with as little as a 20-minute notice.

4.3 Summon the team

Be sure your team alerts you about 30 minutes before they have prototypes ready to review. Put out the notice that you'll be ready to review prototypes in 20 minutes.

Rapid review

This is a fun activity. Everyone will be very interested in seeing the prototype. Reactions can be enthusiastic or disappointing. You should be happiest at either of the extremes. If the group really likes what they see, this is obviously promising for the design. You're going to look

121

at alternatives anyway, but having something that the group likes early in the process will help maintain everyone's willingness to continue.

> ➤ **5.0 Review Prototype 1** ◄

5.1 Team comes to review the prototype created.

5.2 Discuss improvements, possibly brainstorm further approaches, etc. What worked? What didn't?

5.3 Plan next steps. Debrief the prototyping process. What happens next? Who else gets involved? How do we move forward?

If the group really dislikes the prototype, you should also feel that the process is working. The group may fully understand why the process is as powerful as it is when they see that something that sounded very good in discussion didn't turn out so well when it was implemented. The prototyping effort was done quickly, so little time was lost. The group can now identify things that they should avoid, and this is a step forward.

What you'll do next depends, of course, on the outcome.

Although the group would probably be willing to spend much more than the 45 minutes you've allotted, it's important to let the group know upon re-assembly that they should limit this task to less than an hour.

5.1 Team comes to review prototype

Prototypes are barely enough to express the idea. You will need to add plenty of explanation to help everyone imagine what a completed application would look like if this prototype were fully implemented. However, try not to qualify the prototype so much that you're back to presenting a storyboard instead of a functional prototype.

5.2 Discuss improvements

You'll have plenty of flip-chart pages on the wall to help the group remember what they're trying to achieve with the design. Remind them, if necessary, that the learning event must be meaningful to the learners, memorable, and motivational. Take up each of these criteria one at a time, and ask how the design could be made stronger in that area.

Write out lists of what worked and what didn't.

5.3 Plan next steps

Even if the group were highly satisfied with the prototype, the process calls for trying again. That is, we set the prototype aside and challenge the group anew. Ask the group, "If you couldn't do what we did with this prototype, what would we do?"

Groups that are happy with their first prototype are often resistant to this challenge at first. They want to retain many elements of their first prototype and tend to propose a nearly identical design. But as they take on the challenge, perhaps only at your insistence, they often devise something that's so clever and good that it surprises everyone.

Repeat three times

You're now at the point of iterating the process. Design. Prototype. Review.

In general, you'll find that three iterations are enough. The group will probably find that their second iteration produced a superior design, but there are a few elements of their first design that they would like to bring back. The third iteration is often, therefore, something of a blend of the first two prototypes, although it can certainly be something entirely fresh and new—and better!

9.1 Discuss importance of user feedback

Many organizations don't expect to obtain user feedback nor think it would be valuable until after the application is complete and bullet-proof. Everything should be fully intuitive or explained, with support guides and full accoutrements,

before users become involved. Waiting that long, however, prevents taking advantage of user ideas in the design.

It's not only feasible but extremely valuable to hear user responses at the earliest possible moment in the process. There's no reason, in fact, that learners couldn't review prototypes just as productively as the Savvy team does, and this is a review activity you should make happen.

> **6.0 Brainstorm Prototype 2** <

> **7.0 Build Prototype 2** <

> **8.0 Review Prototype 2** <

> **9.0 User Feedback** <

9.1 Discuss importance of user feedback at this point.

9.2 Discuss logistics of obtaining learner feedback

Learners will tell you surprising things. I stressed the value of having a recent learner and/or a targeted learner in the Savvy team itself. If you were able to accomplish this and you found someone willing and able to speak up, you may already be aware of the value you take away from listening to learners. Try as we all do, we cannot fully assume the perspective of a learner and therefore cannot see confusions, opportunities, and needs as they do.

Sometimes learners cannot verbalize what's happening, so it's actually good that you are there with them, explaining that many pieces of the prototype are incomplete, filling in the holes, and describing what the final application would look like. This discussion will help learners talk with you about what they think would and would not be helpful.

You should listen carefully and analytically. Don't take what they say at face value, but rather think why they may have made the comments they did. The information you need isn't just what learners say. Your learners probably aren't professional instructional designers and might very well recommend things that would be ineffective, but understanding what's behind the suggestions they make will often lead to some very good design ideas.

Learners are expert, of course, in what confuses them, what interests them, and what interfaces they can understand and use. If you're tempted to say to a seemingly disinterested learner, "This should interest you because it can make your work easier," you should stop yourself and realize that you haven't made the personal value apparent through your design. Or, perhaps, making their work easier isn't really a goal of your learners.

If you're tempted to say to a frustrated learner, "If you wanted

to check resources before submitting your answer for judgment, you should have clicked this button," you should realize that your design didn't make that option clear.

User reviews provide an important opportunity to ask questions and probe into what might make your design truly successful. Making assumptions about what will and won't work for any given learner population is very tempting indeed. We easily assume that learners will respond much as (we think) we would. But this assumption is often a mistake that causes applications to be ineffective and requires costly redesign to fix. It's much less expensive to verify assumptions and make good early design decisions than it is to make corrections after your application has been fully developed.

Regardless of how sure you are that you've made good assumptions, test them with learners at the prototyping stage. You can be almost guaranteed that you've made some bad ones. Further, you probably made many assumptions you didn't realize you had made. And some of these were probably quite wrong, too. Now is the time to move closer to the right track.

Note that checking designs with users is not a one-time design fix. You will need to retest your designs as they evolve and become more fully fleshed out. For example, learners might indicate or demonstrate their comfort based on a missing element you could only describe with an early prototype. Once that element is actually in place, testing might reveal that it doesn't, and perhaps even can't, have the effect you had described, leaving the learner quite bewildered. Test. Test. Test. And be successful. It really isn't that hard, and it doesn't take that long to do.

9.2 Discuss logistics of obtaining learner feedback

There are logistics to arrange. If it's possible to conduct some review sessions in the evening before the second day of the Savvy Start, this could be very helpful. If not, perhaps it would be possible on the second day or in the evening between the second and third days. If you are working with an organization that has used successive approximations previously, then you probably have the support you need to arrange for user availability. With organizations new to the process, however, they probably need to have the first day's experience before they can imagine the value of involving learners so soon.

It can be helpful to videotape reviews. Learners are sometimes a bit nervous about the camera's presence at first, but they always forget it's there in only a few minutes. If you have access to a user testing lab with one-way mirrors, an observation booth, and/or recording facilities, so much the better, but a very simple, inexpensive arrangement with home recording equipment is fine. If you can conduct recorded reviews overlapping the Savvy Start event, you'll be able to show snippets of the tape to your team. They'll find it incredibly helpful and, no doubt, provide you all the future support you need for user reviews.

12 | The Objectives x Treatments Matrix

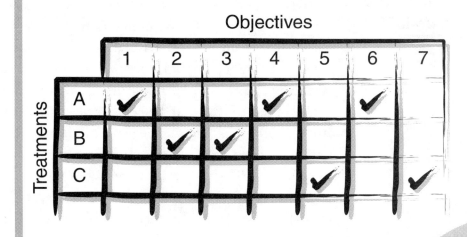

The shortest distance is a curved line

The iterative plan we're using actually defines the shortest distance between the start of a project to create success behaviors and the realization of a program that does just that. The circular path is efficient because so many things are intertwined. We can't keep our eyes on all of the important factors at one time, but we can't afford to ignore any, so we iterate, looking repeatedly at our needs, decisions, and the impact of our tentative decisions on all other factors.

The circular path, exploratory, experimental, fun, and enlightening as it is, could be non-ending. It would not achieve our need to be both effective and efficient with time and resources if we were perpetually stuck in iterations, even if they continued to improve our designs. After the first day of relatively freeform exploration and two prototyping cycles, we need to step back a moment and lay out the path for moving forward.

10.1 Discuss delivery platform

You need to know whether available

> **10.0 Delivery Platform Assessment, and Tracking** ◁

delivery equipment is capable of presenting the media and interactivity your group is scheming up. Can it play sound effects, streaming sound, streaming video, animation, CD-ROMs, audio CDs or DVDs, or whatever else you want?

Although the cost of capable multimedia computers is miniscule in comparison to the cost of wasted learner time and the effects of poorly trained performers, it can be difficult in both corporate and academic institutions to upgrade hardware as necessary to support optimal learning experiences. If your group knows what is and isn't possible, perhaps from your backgrounding data, you can set design constraints immediately. If some flexibility is possible, you can attempt to stay within the capabilities of existing systems at first to see whether they will be adequate. If not, you'll need to explore upgrades.

Don't forget basic networking requirements. Some designs will not be viable if the delivery platform

doesn't have access to high-speed communications or performance data as learners work. For example, if learners will be involved in multi-player games, computers will need to be networked and have uninterrupted access. If the instructional design provides exercises based on each learner's growing competencies, records of the learner's response history must be available to the computer, even if the learner uses a different computer for each session.

10.2 Review goals for assessment

Academic tests are given for multiple purposes. Ideally, they are given to help instructors guide their students. By knowing what strengths and weaknesses exist in individual learners, instructors can determine what learners need to learn and are ready to learn. Because instructors are often working with many learners, however, they aren't often able to craft individual learning plans. Indeed, their instructional plans are often set before the term begins, and learners will need to keep up as best they can.

In reality, most academic tests are seen as measures of learning for record. Grades or marks are recorded and intended to stand as an indication of proficiency. Whether or not they have any validity is open to serious question.

Unfortunately, because grades are recorded, tests have taken on yet another capacity as an incentive to study. Fear of recorded failure. Lovely. A tool that could be most useful for making instruction more effective becomes an anvil raised over learners' heads. It works to a certain degree, but it also results in a uniquely human behavior: learning for a test. Somehow, we manage to put forth enough effort to pass tests and then, rather efficiently from some points of view, purge all that test-learning the moment the anvil is put at rest.

Assess for a purpose

Because your project exists to achieve behavioral change, the most vital, ultimate assessment is whether it achieves that behavioral change. I sometimes like using the assessment anvil to build learner motivation to succeed, but its most effective form is not as a posttest. Rather, as an assessment of on-the-job or in-real-life behavior.

In the school setting, I'm sure any teacher would be more satisfied and proud if a student were able to participate in an intelligent conversation on a subject of instruction with learned individuals than able to write a good test.

In the business setting, I'm sure any trainer would be more satisfied if an employee could correct a mechanical malfunction quickly than if he could write a good test on how it should be done.

10.3 Stipulate assessments

Your team has developed ideas of the instructional events you believe would be valuable, and even some prototypes of them. You should now define clearly how you will measure success.

The multiple types of assessments to be stipulated typically include:

➢ Measures of learning
  • Indicators of strengths and weaknesses that can be used to individualize instruction
  • Learner performance data useful for evaluating the effectiveness of each instructional event
➢ Summative measures of success
  • Indications of applied behavioral changes
  • Measures of related organizational success

An Alternative Approach

Some would argue theoretically, and with merit, that you should define assessments before designing any learning events. Such an approach would assure your assessments are tied to your primary goal, as they should be, and not to learning events, which are only a means to your goal. Experience suggests, however, that the sequence described here is usually more successful in the context of rapid design. There are several reasons for this:

> Getting to the design activities and focusing initially, as we do, on learning events that provide practice of targeted outcome behaviors, keeps the group more energetically awake and involved.

> As groups define exactly the behaviors they want to see learners performing, they are ready to think of assessment in terms of things that truly matter, as opposed to "correctly answering eight out of ten questions about good customer service."

> When groups set assessments first and cement them in place, they sacrifice the benefits of successive approximation (which suggests that several iterative reconsiderations of the goal are better than a one-time attempt at perfection).

10.4 Discuss performance tracking

Collecting data items necessary for specified assessments may require supportive networking and database-management capabilities. There are many creative ways data can be centralized, even if learners are working on un-networked computers most of the time. But watch out for restrictive firewalls or confidentiality issues and policies that may prevent required user log-in or collection of certain data that might be just what you need for an ideal learning activity.

10.5 Determine compliancy issues (if any)

If you are training for certification, building exercises that work with confidential information, or training performance that has significant liabilities (surgical procedures, commercial airline piloting), you'll have compliancy issues. You'll also have compliance issues if the application is going to interface to a learning management or a learning content management system (LMS or LCMS). There may be a need for the application to be accessible to people with disabilities or comply with certain technical standards, such as SCORM or AICC.

Your backgrounding research may be helpful here, but there may still be open questions. See what your Savvy Start team knows or requires, as any information you have will be useful for knowing what options you can consider as you design the application.

10.6 Review the role of formal instructional objectives

Instructional objectives can give

design and development a helpful foundation. We don't start with formally written objectives because the exercise tends to put off people who aren't used to working with them—and because it can be a boring activity. Backgrounding and the first cycles of prototyping begin to reveal a clear sense of what behavioral skills need to be developed.

At this point, however, you may need to explain what instructional objectives are, what makes a useful objective, and why we write them at this point. Note the example objective above and the reminders of how to write objectives below. In the example, you can see that complete behavioral objectives have three components:

1. A description of observable behavior (answer or refer)
2. The conditions under which the learner must be able to perform the behavior (within twenty seconds of answering a customer request call)
3. A description of successful performance (correct at least nine out of ten calls)

Note that verbs such as "think," "understand," and "know" are not observable behaviors, whereas "list,"

Sample behavioral objective

Within twenty seconds of answering a customer request call, hotline personnel will make no more than one error in ten calls when determining whether they can and should answer the incoming question or make a referral.

"identify," and "complete" are. Even if it's our intent to stimulate cognitive functions, such as appreciating, understanding, or feeling, it's important for us to express observable manifestations of this hidden behavior so that we can assess whether or not our instruction is having the needed impact.

11.0 Write Objectives

Once the group has worked through some prototypes, it actually becomes a refreshing task to write out objectives. We'll need the objectives for estimating the amount of work to be done, preparing cost estimates, listing needed resources, setting out a project schedule, and, in short, doing many of the project planning tasks ahead.

You could still be thinking that it's a little late to be writing objectives. It certainly is different from what

> ▷ **11.0 Write Objectives** ◁

11.1 Review the organization's goal; restate if appropriate.

11.2 Write one or two objectives.

11.3 Discuss resources and responsibilities. Who is going to analyze behaviors the Savvy Start team won't address and write corresponding objectives? How will consensus be achieved for these additional course objectives?

we advocate in other approaches. Objectives are important, very important, as we'll see later. But writing them too soon tends to put a damper on the design process. It tends to focus designers on artificial aspects of learning solutions rather than on real-world interests and needs.

In successive approximation, we alternate between points of great inventive freedom and tightly focused tasks. This tactic not only produces more creative and effective solutions, but it makes the design process more fun and energetic. We began with identifying the overall goal and then jumped immediately to a few creative solutions. This activity probably helped the team scrutinize the goal and achieve a bit more clarity as well as some broader perspectives. Now it's time to narrow the focus.

11.1 Review the organization's goal; restate if appropriate

Check once again the stated reason the organization is developing this training. What do they hope to achieve and why? Now that the Savvy Team is getting a deepening sense of what can be accomplished, might they want to fine-tune the goal? It's not too late, and it's a good time to double-check.

11.2 Write one or two objectives

An important use of objectives is to determine how many prototypes will be needed for designing the entire application. We do this by preparing a matrix of objectives and the instructional designs we selected or created. See the sample Objectives x Treatments Matrix on page 133.

Objectives 1 and 2 can be reached by using the same context. You need to develop only one prototype for each different context and for each different type of activity during the Savvy Start.

If you write objectives in the left column of a three-column table (as shown), you'll be able to fill in the table as you develop prototypes. As you take up successive objectives, you can look to see whether you have a context and an activity that would constitute a good learning event. If so, you can simply note that you will reuse existing designs here and move on to other objectives.

This exercise will be instructive to your team, and it will help them see how objectives are used to estimate the amount of effort it will take to complete the entire project. At this point in the process, however, it's not necessary to write the full complement of objectives, even if you could. Just write a few so that you can select a couple for prototyping and demonstrate the process that will be continued later.

11.3 Discuss resources and responsibilities

This may or may not be a good time to consider a short discussion on who will be responsible for writing objectives. If there are people in the room who clearly understand the process and also the goals and prerequisite behaviors, it could be a great time to get the group's support for their taking this important responsibility.

Objectives x Treatments Matrix

Objective	Treatment	
	e-Learning Context	e-Learning Activity
1. Learner will correctly describe, five out of six times, one of the Motorola phone's top five features as an advantage over another vendor's phone of interest to a customer.	Context A: Simulated phone sales kiosk Customer selects a phone.	From an extensive list of possible phone capabilities, learner clicks one that is (1) a top five feature of the selected Motorola phone and (2) not a feature of the competitor's phone.
2. Learner will correctly select, ten out of ten times in a row, a Motorola phone that has a requested feature.	Context A: Simulated phone sales kiosk Customer asks for a phone that has a specific feature.	Learner clicks on correct phone image among a set of at least four phones.
3. Learner will correctly order the steps of pairing a Bluetooth-equipped phone at least three times in a row.	Context B: Simulated phone with click-able buttons	Learner clicks phone buttons to set up communications options, enter pass code, and reach "Pairing Completed" message.

It may be a responsibility your team can and should take, and if so, you could explain this function now and seek support. If it looks like this will be a difficult and lengthy discussion, simply note that a resolution on this will be needed before a project plan can be put together. And move on.

12.0 — 17.0 Brainstorm, prototype, and review

Develop two more prototypes following the same procedures as before.

13 | Assessing Context and Constraints

On this, the third day of the Savvy Start, we review what we've done, what we've learned, and what we want to do. Bringing everything together as a basis for planning the remaining work and achieving a plan that's directly on target and has full support of the key stakeholders is the primary purpose of the entire event. If the process has gone quickly, there's even a bonus. There'll be time to build another prototype.

18.0 Prototypes in context

The final application is much more than the prototypes, of course. There will be an overall context with navigation to help learners access exercises. There will probably be a number of learner support tools also, such as a reference glossary, notebook, links for discussions, and email addresses to make contact with others and ask questions. If you're developing a blended solution, you will have been talking about how the prototyped lessons or interactions fit with and support other learning activities and how other activities will support the e-learning. The critical interdependencies of all learning activities will be mapped out in

Rapid reader

- Use prototypes to help clarify the big picture, together with its needs and constraints.

- Prototyped ideas need to become blueprints of learning events that are practical to create, implement, and deliver.

- Assignment of responsibilities helps project managers project realistic costs and schedules.

much more detail as the complete solution is designed.

18.1 Review remaining process

Before you continue with prototyping, this is probably an excellent time to help the team consider what happens after today, when the Savvy Start has concluded. Team members may be concerned that they haven't been able to cover all the targeted behaviors, or that there must be many other design issues that they haven't addressed. It's time to put these concerns, if there are any, to rest. And it's helpful to refresh the context of the Savvy Start within the overall process.

After the Savvy Start has been completed, there is a good basis for estimating how much the entire project is going to cost, what resources will need to be available, and how long it's going to take. Many organizations want to know this, of course, even before they undertake a Savvy Start, but it's truly impossible to know. That's like asking a builder for an estimate of how much it will cost to build a custom home without knowing what the building site is like, how many rooms the house is to have, what style and level of finish it is to have, and so on. The range of possible costs is simply too large to have any value. The Savvy Start provides answers that, together with backgrounding information, a commitment of critical resources (such as SMEs, supervisors, and learners), and the new prototypes, narrow the range of possible costs and make it possible to provide well-founded estimates.

A red flag should be raised when cost and other estimates are given without input from a Savvy Start. Of course, it's possible to build learning solutions at a very wide range of cost points, but the solutions are not going to have equal effectiveness. Solutions that are underbid are likely to be so ineffective that the entire investment is wasted. Learner time will be wasted, and opportunities will be lost. Learners may develop a dislike for the content area or decide they have insufficient aptitude and dramatically change their future plans. Launching an ineffective program is damaging and expensive.

> ▷ **18.0 Prototypes in Context** ◁

18.1 Review the process for creating the complete application (completion of Objectives x Treatments Matrix, integrating prototypes, number of cycles needed, integrating media, and developing the alpha, beta, and gold versions).

18.2 Discuss need for and means of gathering user feedback.

The next step is to prepare a project plan. This will probably take from three days to two weeks, depending on the size of the project and how much additional information needs to be gathered. The first step will be to complete the Objectives x Treatments Matrix, as this determines how many different treatments are to be developed and how much content material will have to be prepared.

To review the entire process at a high level, which is something you should probably do now with the entire team, here is the sequence.

1. Backgrounding
2. Savvy Start
3. Project plan
4. Additional prototyping
5. Design proof
6. Alpha application development
7. Beta application development
8. Final (gold) application development

Although it may look complex, it's really only the one structure of design, development, and evaluation repeated at different levels. We study what is needed, create a possible solution, and evaluate it in the most efficient way possible.

18.2 Discuss need for and means of gathering user feedback

What gives you assurance that the process will yield a successful result? Frequent evaluation. Much of the evaluation requires the availability of learners to try the evolving application. It can be difficult to orchestrate, but the value is so great that you really must find the means.

It's likely the Savvy Start team sees the value of feedback from learners from the experience they've had with rapid prototyping. Even if the person with the authority to arrange learner availability isn't in the room, the support you develop for learner feedback will probably help you make arrangements later. Be sure to identify who you need to work with and any problems that you might anticipate.

19.0 The perfect solution

One of the theoretical underpinnings of successive approximation is the notion that no design or training solution is perfect. Ever. All designs and programs can be made better, but any attempt to realize perfection is futile and unaffordable. The process therefore promotes small steps of experimentation. No step consumes so much of the project's

➤ 19.0 The Perfect Solution ◄

19.1 Describe the perfect solution, given your conversations throughout the previous two days regarding need, analysis, gap, potential solutions, tracking, assessments, etc.:

- What items would it track?

- How would you know learners gained knowledge and experience?

- What kind of reporting data would it generate?

- How would it be accessed, and what type of security would be present?

19.2 Discuss who is best prepared to contribute to the ideal solution. Who, for example, can contribute not only content expertise, but also learning and performance inspiration?

resources that the output of any step cannot be discarded if it is determined to be ineffective.

Each successive approximation is undertaken to move our work closer to the ideal (without the foolish expectation of actually getting there). In order for us to judge whether an iteration is effective, we need to have some sense of what the perfect solution might be. Please note that, in line with this reasoning, we cannot even expect our definition of the ideal solution to be perfect. And this is why those of us using the process must expect shifts in our understanding of almost everything as we repetitively experiment with designs. It couldn't be otherwise.

19.1 Describe the perfect solution

Having explored some solutions, the team should have a better sense of what's possible and what would work within their organization.

You've looked at the project's target a number of times, always maintaining focus on the overall goal of organizational and individual success. Now try one more perspective on defining the goal.

How will the application tell you whether it has accomplishing what you need it to accomplish? This is feedback you'll need as the training is put into use. This tells you what's happening.

What information do you want to know as learners work through the learning experiences? Do you want to know what errors they make, what comments they have, what options or tools they use?

What evidence can the application provide that learning has occurred? What evidence can be collected that learners are able to apply their learning?

What kinds of reports do you want? Who needs them and when do they need them? Can some individual performance data be used to help mentors? What performance data needs to be kept private? How secure does it need to be?

While all these questions need to be answered for cost estimates and the project plan to be completed, this is a discussion that can be helpful in designing your solution.

19.2 Discuss who will do what

You're getting closer and closer to a project plan. You need to identify the ideal team and then, very pragmatically, learn who is and is not going to be able take responsibilities for continuing roles. Watch out for delegation that removes real decision-makers from the process. This often causes major problems because the person who steps back and isn't involved closely may retain the power to veto decisions made by his or her delegate. When people do not fully understand why decisions were made, vetoes can cause problematic delays and/or poor direction.

20.0 Project constraints

As a complement to the ideal solution, you need to know what will be realistic. Every project has constraints it must work within and other constraints that can be relaxed if and when warranted. It helps if you know which are which.

20.1 Budget and timeline

You're going to determine what would be the most appropriate budget for the project based on the Savvy Start and all the other information collected. You want to be sure, of course, that it's worth going forward and putting in all the time and effort that are necessary to create a sound, responsible proposal.

Unless you've had a lot of experience in developing learning applications, it would be unwise to now hazard a guess of the budget necessary for what's being laid out. There's a lot of information for you to process in arriving at such a determination.

At this point, the group should be quite sure of the learning experiences necessary to achieve the outcomes they need. Hopefully, they are also convinced that doing something ineffective will be the most costly path they can take. It will be unfortunate if they have a predetermined budget locked in place that's too small, but if they do, your best course of action will be to recommend a phased approach in which each part of the solution can be done well enough to achieve its intended goal.

It is important to know what cost expectations exist, if any. If the

> **▷ 20.0 Project Constraints ◁**

20.1	Budget and timeline
20.2	SME access and content
20.3	Project teams, approvals, decision-making

decision-maker thinks it looks like a $25,000 project, and it's clear from the prototyping work that the group is moving toward something upward of $100,000, you'll want to discuss this problem right away, introduce the notion of a phased approach, and determine how you want to proceed.

Similarly, you want to be sure there's a reasonable expectation of a timeline. While some e-learning projects can be completed in just a few days, many take several months. If there's a very short timeline, you'll want to discuss whether resources exist for rapid content preparation, rapid reviews, and rapid approvals. You might want to discuss parallel design and development efforts with multiple teams working on different modules of instruction concurrently.

20.2 SME access and content

Experts are often very busy people. Those who hold the standards for an organization's best practices and those most esteemed for both their knowledge and teaching abilities in educational institutions are often busy with an extraordinary workload. While these very people are often among the most enthusiastic supporters of training development,

their involvement in a time-sensitive project is often problematic. Development teams frequently list delayed access to SMEs and delayed approvals as the primary causes of budget and schedule overruns.

Discuss what content currently exists and in what form it exists. Content developed for one form of instructional delivery, such as instructor-led classroom learning, is not sufficient for interactive instruction, where the development of learning experiences that provide learners the opportunities to make mistakes and and receive helpful feedback requires much more content depth.

20.3 Project teams, approvals, decision-making

With your team assembled, and the experience they will have gained by the end of these three days, you have a group that is uniquely prepared to help your project succeed. You want to keep them involved and assigned to tasks that fit their abilities. You've also had a chance to witness each person's style of contribution, and that will give you some thoughts about how you'd like to work with him or her.

Talk about teaming. Suggest how you'd like to work together and see what prospects you have for getting the support you want. Their willingness to cooperate will be another factor that's important to consider as you develop your schedule and budget.

Most important are the issues of getting approvals and decisions made. It's easy for an organization to demand delivery of a learning application at a certain time, such as at school opening in the fall or the scheduled time of a new product launch, but then delay the timely completion of reviews and approvals. Talking about this now won't necessarily prevent problems ahead, but you want to raise awareness and gain a commitment to provide the support necessary.

If the scope of the project changes, who will approve the changes and any budgetary ramifications, if any? If an approval is late, who has the authority to obtain it or approve a change to the project budget and schedule? Get all the answers you can now, while project enthusiasm is high and no project problems are on the table.

21.0 Media

Sound effects, music, narration, graphics, illustrations, photographs, video, and animation are important tools for creating learning experiences with impact. They are often indispensable for creating an affective impact on the learner, which, in turn, can heighten learner motivation and learning retention.

> **➤ 21.0 Media ◄**

> 21.1 Present a variety of applications using different approaches to media. Discuss pros and cons of different styles.
> 21.2 Gather feedback and opinions on what defines the desired look and feel.
> 21.3 Discuss sound, video, animation . . . anything that can impact performance of running WBT.

But media are also selected, used, and styled for many other reasons. The culture of an organization determines how much the aesthetics of a design are valued. Sometimes strict media guidelines exist.

The fidelity of the media can indicate how much importance the organization puts on the training and/or the related product or service.

Although the quality of a training application ought to be determined solely by its ability to produce the desired behaviors, there's no doubt that it is often judged by how it looks. Learners have more positive expectations of e-learning that has visual appeal, a positive spirit, and engaging energy. So media are definitely of value. They can also greatly influence the cost of a project.

21.1 Present a variety of applications

Describing media treatments just doesn't convey enough information. You need to show different levels and types of treatments to have a constructive discussion. Groups often find it's appropriate to design and develop prototypes, using the same design—prototype—review process we've been using, to determine the media guidelines to be followed. You might want a media prototype to be your next prototyping activity.

➢ 22.0 Brainstorm Prototype 5 ◁

22.1 New content or build off an existing prototype? Depends on what's needed.

22.2 Integrate anything that comes up during the "comprehensive solution" approach.

➢ 23.0 Build Prototype 5 ◁

➢ 24.0 Review Prototype 5 ◁

21.2 Gather feedback and opinions

There may be very divergent opinions within your group, but see if there's a style the group likes and feels is important. If you cannot detect a clear direction on this, be sure to ask who will make the ultimate decision. Then see whether you can get the group to agree on the three things they most want and the three things they most definitely don't want. If they can agree, you'll have some useful guidance, if not a clear mandate.

21.3 Discuss sound, video, animation

Your group may want extensive use of media that will strain their delivery bandwidth. While some in-house networks are ready and capable of handling full-screen, high-fidelity streaming video and sound, for example, dial-up Internet users aren't going to have the same experience. Make sure the group isn't quickly setting unrealistic expectations you can't solve within the development of your application.

22.0 – 24.0 Brainstorm, prototype, and review Prototype 5

There may be time for one more prototype. You should select the topic based on the top questions that have come up in your discussions. It might be that this should be your media or look-and-feel prototype. It might be that this should be another iteration on a previously prototyped concept. It might be that a new target behavior has been identified that seems unusually difficult to teach. You probably won't have any trouble coming up with candidates; the problem will be in deciding which one to take up. Vote?

25.0 Final strategy review

It's time to wrap up. If things went well, everyone's outlook for the project is high, but everyone is tired too. These sessions keep people focused and thinking hard over a long period of time, and it takes a toll on their energy. Still, a good wrap-up affects how productive people will feel the event was.

25.1 Review project risks

Take the time to use your flip chart. Label the page "Project Risks." Divide it into three columns, labeled successively as Risk, Prevention, Resource. Ask the group to identify the risks they see. Then indicate in the next columns what actions they feel can help prevent that risk and what resource should be enlisted to help resolve it, if the problem occurs.

25.2 Discuss the project plan

You might want to distribute just an outline, but either an outline or a sample plan will help set expecta-tions. It might also bring out a few important questions. (We'll discuss project plans in detail in another book in the series.)

25.3 Discuss final questions

Turning the group's attention to the Savvy Start process; ask if they felt this was a productive process and how they feel about the direction for the project that their efforts created. This process works very, very well in almost every instance, so you're likely to get very positive responses. Positive or not, however, there may well be some concerns about how some issues will be handled. In three days, you obviously couldn't cover everything, let alone settle every issue.

Thank everyone for their partici-pation, and let them know that their work will be a cornerstone for the success of this project. They will be receiving frequent communications from you (or a designated person), and as future prototypes are devel-oped, their input will be sought and welcomed.

And now you've done it! The Savvy Start.

> **25.0 Final Strategy Review** ◁

25.1 Review project risks.

25.2 Discuss what to expect in the project plan.

25.3 Discuss any final questions about next steps, the process as a whole.

14 | Completing Design, Planning Development

More iterations

I have something important to reveal to you now that will ease a concern you may have. The Savvy Start is actually just a start. Unless the project is very small or it happens that a single learning context will suffice for all learning events, such as a simulated machine or a bank teller's station, there's no way your team will complete the design and prototyping needed for the full project in just two or three days. And it isn't necessary to.

The Savvy Start has many purposes, as we've already discussed, not the least of which is to get vital information on the table,

stakeholders in support, and a design direction established that will allow you to discuss budgets, schedules, and alternatives. The objective isn't really to do as much design work as possible, although every bit of design detail that has enthusiastic support is helpful going forward, so don't worry about that.

More design and prototyping work will need to be done after the Savvy Start has been completed. You should have enough direction and support from the blue rib-

яapid reader

- The Savvy Start synchronizes expectations and provides a basis for planning.

- A project plan, schedule, and budget can be prepared now (and really couldn't have been earlier).

- Content development is a challenging task.

- There is usually too much existing content to use and not enough of the necessary content.

bon team you've assembled for the Savvy Start that a smaller group will be able to carry on in a consistent direction without everyone's participation. In addition, you'll have a project plan, so future design work can be more narrowly focused.

Special-purpose prototypes

Long before an integrated application is available for review, it is important to thoroughly test a variety of designs and technical components, such as the interface to a learning management system (LMS), the performance of media on the actual delivery platform to be used, and styling of displays. Once again, special purpose prototypes come to the rescue. Special-purpose prototypes are an effective and efficient way of squaring away these important items early in the process. And early is good.

In some cases, you'll actually need to fit a few prototypes together to create a mini course just for the purpose of testing. Testing the interface to an LMS, for example, usually requires creation of a mini course, because the evolving application cannot typically be kept connected to a live LMS. Even if it were connected, it would be difficult to test

a developing course because access and flow logic would be restricted by LMS functions that control access and sequencing of events. Since waiting until the application is completed is waiting much too long to check LMS interconnection functionality, a mini course or specialized prototype is the answer.

The Savvy Start summary report

During the Savvy Start there is a concentrated time of exploration, design, rapid prototyping, and review of the possible design of the project. During this time together, the team may redefine the targeted behavioral outcomes and even target a different or enlarged learner group. It may well recommend a phased approach to the introduction of new learning events as a means of making everything easier to control and having the advantage of fully testing the recommended instructional approach before investing too much.

Prototypes are used in successive approximation for many reasons. Chief among them is that alternatives, such as storyboards and specification documents, are open to misinterpretation. Agreements founded on misinterpretations early in the process erupt into missed expectations, refused sign-offs, budget overruns, and other disasters later in the process as development work produces functional applications. For this reason, it is important to continue to build on prototypes as a way of communicating design directions and decisions, as opposed to voluminous documents.

Prototypes do not include all of the elements that are essential for a project plan, of course. And it is important to confirm the principles derived from Savvy Start discussions and prototypes to help assure there is truly an agreement on the direction to be taken. The design details should therefore be summarized in a Savvy Summary Report that becomes the basis of the project plan. Included in the report are often the following items:

> **Solution Strategy.** This includes the targeted behavioral objectives and descriptions of who will use the learning application, the learning events planned, and why these specific events were chosen as the means of developing the needed behavioral changes.

> **General Design Principles.** The general design principles list the key features that the application must have or avoid. For example, "The word *test* is never to be used, and progress assessments are to be embedded within ongoing exercises and games to avoid the test sensitivity that exists among our learners."

> **Instructional Design.** The summary report describes the primary paradigms that will be used to achieve meaningful, memorable, and motivational learning. It will describe how learner interest will be maximized, how the instruction will adapt to learner needs, and how proficiency will be assured.

> **Interface Design.** Prototypes can speak to this issue more fully and easily than documents in many cases, but additional documentation may be necessary to describe accessibility, needed compliance with standards or other media used in a blended solution, and platform compatibility.

> **Scope and Sequence.** While the objectives list can be used to define the scope, it's quite likely that prototyping done during the Savvy Start did not fully address sequencing issues. It may not be necessary to define this until after

further design work has been done, but if sequencing issues were discussed during the Savvy Start, it may be appropriate to capture those thoughts, concerns, and/or agreements here.

Initial media and content style guides

Because consistency of style is essential, and also because the level of media treatments selected affects development costs, it is important to create style guides for media and content prior to developing an overall project budget and plan. The guides can and should define styles in large part by reference to specific applications or a collection of exemplary specimens, including project prototypes, rather than an attempt to write out lengthy descriptive documents.

Guides constructed immediately after the Savvy Start can only be initial guides, however, as more design work will be done once the full design and development project has commenced. The guides will most likely need to be refined, if not changed significantly, as additional prototyping work is completed and needs are defined.

Initial media and content development plans

A major expense in any e-learning project is the development of the media and content. It's easy to underestimate the amount of work that needs to be done here and the talent needed to do it well. Poor content, of course, ruins the application and prevents a successful learning outcome.

The three top challenges instructional designers list when asked about the most difficult problems they face in producing the quality of product they feel is appropriate are:

1. Dealing with an overwhelming amount of content
2. Having access to key people at the times their input, review, or sign-off is needed
3. Coming up with creative designs that fully engage the audience and achieve the needed behavioral changes

I'll attempt to deal with items 2 and 3 elsewhere in this book series. With regard to the first item, there is a great temptation to think that a clear presentation of content will achieve a lot. It doesn't do that much, of course. People have to put new information to work in a meaningful context in order to learn much of anything. In fact, to have maximum impact, it's best to reduce the volume of content as much as possible and focus on a few key points. But when a lot of content exists, organizations often want to use it all—insist on using it all—even when it's contrary to their better judgment.

This figure provides a graphic view of a typical content development process for an e-learning project.

The frustrating fact is that there is typically both too much existing content to use (represented by the dark wedge on the left) and not enough that's appropriate to use. To achieve behavioral change, we need to create meaningful, memorable, and motivational experiences. Most existing material cannot simply be reused because it is not focused on the learner or the learning experience. It almost never has the specific components (contexts, challenges, activities, and feedback) needed to build interactive learning events.

As the figure shows, the process of content development begins with identifying existing raw materials and paring them down to what is usable in an interactive setting. Some of it, if not much of it, can be used as resources learners can access at their option, but it shouldn't be presented to all learners verbatim on the screen in lieu of compelling

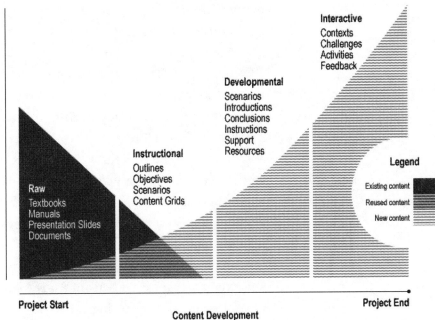

learning experiences.

If instructional materials exist, such as outlines or objectives used to structure instructor-led delivery or self-study programs, a greater portion of this material is likely to be fitting and useful. Still, much new structural material will need to be developed for the new learning events you are creating.

Finally, there is the large bulk of new content material that must be created, including contexts, challenges, activities, feedback, and much more. This material is voluminous, often becoming even greater in volume than the raw material because interactive programs need much more content than simple presentations ever contain.

Why is this? Presentations do not respond to learner errors, queries, or varying needs for examples and practice, and therefore don't need and don't have the content with which to do it. In highly interactive and individualized programs, no learner is likely to see all of the available material, only what's needed to provide the right learning activity and experience for each person. And yet to provide these learning experiences, a rich library of material must be available for program logic to draw from.

Developing appropriate text and media components is a major undertaking that is much more difficult than you might expect. The development plan needs to identify who is going to undertake this task. *Note:* It's important that this task be assigned to someone who is both talented and qualified to undertake it. Many projects experience overruns because the content has required redevelopment one or more times.

Experience is important here. If you have neither experienced e-learning content and media developers nor the option of contracting the services of such people, it's usually better to select talented writers, artists, and media producers than subject-matter experts for this job. If the people you select have teaching experience, so much the better. It seems easier to become familiar with specific content than it is to learn the art of turning information into powerful learning experiences.

An initial development plan states who you expect to develop the content and media development, as well as an educated guess, based on the Objectives x Treatments Matrix, of how much material will be needed. If inexperienced people are doing the work, you'll want to allow a considerable amount of time for development and revision.

Sample Project Plan Table of Contents

Business Problem
- Organization's Understanding of the Situation
- Operational/Business Impact
- Definition of Success

Concise Statement of Performance Gap

Performance Objectives
- Initial Objectives x Treatments Matrix

Solution Summary

e-Learning/Blended Learning Approach Summary
- Deployment
- Media Assets to Be Included
- Transfer of Training Support

Interactivity Summary
- List of Interactive Treatments Prototyped
- Estimate of Additional Treatments Needed
- Budget Allowance for Additional Treatments

Scenario and Content Development Plan
- Content to Be Provided by Organization
- Content to Be Created by Development Team
- Format of Provided Content

Delivery of Learning Materials
- e-Learning Technical Specification
- Classroom Materials Specification
- Supervisor Materials Specification

Assessment and Tracking Specification (Including LMS Interface)

User Testing Plan

Master Schedule and Deliverables Matrix
- Deliverables Itemization — Proof, Alpha, Beta, Gold Releases
- Responsibility
- Sign-Offs Required
- Date Required

Change Request Process

Quality Assurance Plan

Roles and Decision Making

Communications Plan

Risk and Contingency Management Plan

The project plan

When we take up project management in a companion volume, we'll talk in detail about putting together a comprehensive project plan based on input from the Savvy Start. A sample table of contents is included here to give you a sense of what this document entails.

Additional design

As your team probably discovered, three iterations of the design—prototype—review cycle are often optimal for designing each learning event. Within three iterations, you can agree on what looks promising and what just didn't work out, and you can produce prototypes that will direct additional design and development in compliance with the team's wishes.. More cycles may improve a design a bit, but with each additional iteration, you'll find diminishing returns.

It's unusual for a Savvy Start to cover all the design treatments needed to cover all objectives. There are probably some designs that were reached through a single cycle and should go through the process one or two more times. And there are probably some objectives for which no design was developed. If this is

the case, your project plan will show an incomplete Objectives x Treatments Matrix and call for additional rapid prototyping activities to complete it.

Additional design work follows the same principles and a similar process as was used for the Savvy Start, although the focus can be narrower. You've settled on the target audiences, how success will be defined and measured, and what scope of behaviors you will address. Efficiency is now of increased importance.

Breadth-over-depth principle

Each of the defined learning objectives needs to be assigned one or more instructional treatments that will typically include instruction, practice, and assessment components. Your job now is to design a complete set of instructional events that will cover all objectives. It is typical that some of your designs will be used for multiple objectives, providing both development economies and event familiarity for learners.

Because you are now rounding out the design, you need to keep the whole of the learning application in mind while you design and refine its components. It is important that your different designs maintain interface consistencies and that you provide meaningful transitions as you move from one context to another. This wasn't a major concern in the Savvy Start, so I have a new principle to help you here. It's called the *breadth-over-depth principle.*

Whereas, in the Savvy Start, you stayed focused on an identified behavioral outcome as you prototyped three alternative designs, each better than the previous one, you should now limit yourself on both time and iterations before moving on to the next open objective. Cover all objectives before coming back around to refine your first set of prototypes.

Think of your objectives as the cups in a cupcake pan. Pour some dough in each one, then come back around and even them out with another layer. Bake them, and then put the icing on as a finishing touch. The image of doing this, as opposed to filling one cup full, baking it, and icing it before starting all over with the next cup might be helpful to you as you monitor your work.

You should avoid refining designs before looking at other objects because, as you move across objectives, it's likely you'll see design elements that can be shared if designed for that purpose. Because you have planned to revisit all your designs and haven't finalized any of them, you'll work efficiently to create designs that are consistent and have broad utility.

15 | Develop—Implement—Evaluate

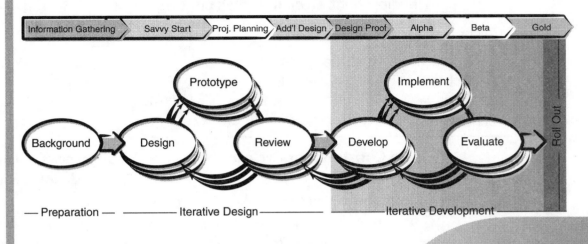

We turn now to the final phase of the process, in which the prototyped designs guide the development of deliverable learning events. Once again, through an iterative approach, we check our work repeatedly.

As the process diagram (above) indicates, three cycles listed are anticipated with time and resources reserved for at least four cycles. Each cycle produces a specific, well-defined product: The Design Proof, Alpha Release, Beta Release, and Gold Release—the finished product.

The Beta Release is a candidate to become the final or Gold Release; the other products are interim steps

to be sure development remains on the right track.

Experience suggests that it is sometimes necessary to make another round of corrections after the Beta Release. It's always better to plan for more development iterations than are needed than to need more than are planned. Corrections themselves sometimes introduce new problems that are not discovered until the application is put into use. So you should always plan for at least one correction iteration—and maybe even two.

Яapid reader

- Development uses iterative cycles very similar to the design cycles.

- Four cycles are anticipated:

  ▲ Construction,
  ▲ Production,
  ▲ Validation, and
  ▲ Correction.

- Each cycle produces a corresponding release for review and QA:

  ▲ Design Proof,
  ▲ Alpha Release,
  ▲ Beta Release, and
  ▲ Gold Release.

Development Cycles and Products

Cycle	Product
Construction	Design Proof
Production	Alpha Release
Validation	Beta Release and Gold Candidate 1
Correction	Gold Candidate 2… N

The Construction Cycle and Design Proof

The Construction Cycle is the first major development effort. It produces the Design Proof—an intentionally incomplete release that brings all the pieces of the design together for the first time. It's an important check to be sure expectations are being met and that the approach will work as a whole. Most importantly, the Design Proof is offered in hopes of rooting out problems as early as possible. Content and media development are limited so that if any change of direction occurs, minimal amounts of work will have been wasted.

The Design Proof is typically characterized as follows:

➤ All structural components are present and functional, including navigation and at least one interaction of every type designed for the course.

➤ Sample graphics and other media are included at final resolution, but placeholders remain for the majority of instances.

➤ Sample content will be included for each major content area and be complete for at least one instance of each different instructual treatment. Otherwise, placeholders will be in place.

➤ Navigation and interactivity structures will collect sample performance data sufficient to test data collection and interconnectivity to external data files or an LMS.

Pseudo functionality

At least one instance of every designed function should be working in the Design Proof, because problems and opportunities can arise, during development and when evaluating application effectiveness. Identifying these problems and opportunities sooner rather than later is quite helpful.

But it's also valuable to release the Design Proof as soon as possible to maximize the development time available between this release and the Alpha Release. Waiting for the development of some complex code might not be smart. Sometimes there has to be a judgment call on whether to hold off release of the Design Proof to complete the development of a function or to go ahead with pseudo functionality—functionality that works only under very specific conditions as a demonstration of concept.

Getting the Design Proof out may be of greater value than unrestricted functionality, especially if you can fake enough functionality so that evaluators can determine the overall value of the integrated design. Functions that will search for and display resource documents, for example, might simply call up a pre-selected file in the Design Proof. However, if this function is part of a simulated problem-solving task, you might be sure it is fully operational so that evaluators can assess the level of behavioral challenge, the effectiveness of the simulation, and the extensiveness of content needed in the resource database.

Development and use of models

Teams that develop many e-learning applications see some functions or structures reoccurring with sufficient frequency to warrant developing reusable models or templates so that they don't have to redevelop the same structure repeatedly. Models can be used for something as trivial as a multiple-choice question or as sophisticated as a multi-player game. They can be terrific for rapid prototyping if an available model happens to match a design idea very closely.

There are advantages and disadvantages of using models. Some approaches to "rapid authoring" tools are actually based on providing a large library of models that can be fit together to make an entire application. This approach is alluring and has been explored for some decades now, generally with less success than hoped.

The problem is that while, indeed, even very complex learning events can be seen as a collection of simple presentations and interactions, the components are complexly integrated in ways that require unique engineering. In addition, display management is simple when only one type of interaction is active at a time, but when multiple interactions need to be active simultaneously, as is often the case for the more interesting learning events, a considerable amount of design and logic needs to be wrestled with to coordinate them.

In the end, it's often easier just to develop cleanly from scratch. The notable exception is when a larger-scale model can be built that provides an engaging interactive context, has the many complex issues worked out both in design and in actual implementation, and draws content from external files. In these cases, models have been shown to be of great value. They reduce development time and allow content developers to build much of the application without programming or scripting. See table Use of Models for some pros and cons of using models.

The decision of when to use models depends on many factors, as is obvious from the list of pros and cons. Also to be considered, of course, is the expected applicability of a model. If a given interaction is to be used many times in one application or many times across multiple applications, then creation of a model has greatly increased advantages.

Use of Models

Pros	Cons
Saves implementation time and cost once built	Requires up-front investment to build
Can be used by non-technical content developers	Requires advanced expertise to design and build
Easier and faster to make global changes	Difficult to create and manage exceptions
Allows pre-testing functionality to eliminate bugs and reduce risks	Requires a stable, well-defined design prior to engineering
Typically reduces file size	At odds with the need for preserving design flexibility throughout project development
Allows multiple content developers to work in tandem (even simultaneously with model development)	Tends to dictate instructional design

From the viewpoint of creating e-learning that will have the greatest impact, it's important to determine first what activities will be the best use of the learners' time. Because there will probably be many learners spending their time with your application, a small economy in development that inefficiently uses learner time is not a wise tradeoff. Be sure not to make a poor judgment here by using the wrong models just because they are available.

Content development

Except for very small learning applications, content development benefits from following a well-defined and structured process—something like filling in the blanks. My studios often create what they call a content grid with component templates.

The grid lists each of the different types of interactions or learning events in the application across the top as column headers. Each use of the event is listed on the left to create labeled rows. Each cell created by the columns and rows represents one instantiation of the event for which content will be needed.

The person assigned to create the needed content, the date by which it is needed, and the status of content

Content Grid: Sexual Harassment Project

Application	Interaction Type			
	Simulated email	Branching dialog	Choice w/ verification	Error elimination
Introductory experience	Template/version: EmailSlim-3	Template/version: Multichoice, bidirect seq-4c	Template/version:	Template/version:
	Author: Karen	Author: Karen	Author:	Author:
	Due by: April 6	Due by: April 6	Due by:	Due by:
	Status: Ready for review	Status: 70%	Status:	Status:
	Comments: Wake up call for mangers that consequnces of errors regarding discrimination and harassment may be frightening.	Comments: Opening experience should help learners realize that common sense approaches won't suffice.	Comments:	Comments:
Module 1	Template/version:	Template/version: Multichoice, bidirect seq-4c	Template/version: 2-step verify-101	Template/ver; Erroe out
	Author:	Author: Karen	Author:	Au

fills in the grid cells. A template is used to specify all the content elements that will be needed for the event, and it's often possible that the content can be provided in the form of a structured spreadsheet that can be automatically read by the application without further manual processing. An additional benefit of this approach is that corrections to content can be made easily by modifying only spreadsheet information.

For the purposes of the Design Proof, it's important that only the structure is created and content written for only a few instructional events to demonstrate the functionality of a design.

Design Proof evaluation

The Design Proof evaluation is perhaps the most important distinct evaluation event in the process. Because all the pieces are coming together as a whole, it's possible to get the clearest sense of what the overall solution is becoming. And yet, there is time to make some corrections, if clearly needed. While much of the programming has been completed, most of the content and media are yet to be developed.

Perhaps most important is to be sure the key decision-maker does not delegate this evaluation, but becomes involved again personally. It won't take a lot of time, but sitting this one out and coming back in later to express surprise, disappointment, or any change in direction can truly be problematic. Would-be delegates are certainly welcome to participate in the evaluation,

but not to the exclusion of the prime decision-maker.

As with all evaluations, you will want to be sure at least a few learners work with the application and give you feedback. You will also want other individuals representing the organization to review the Design Proof. Using a Design Proof Evaluation Checklist (See example on page 162) is a checklist that will assist reviewers in giving the feedback you need.

Bonus babies

Note the arrows returning from iterative development to the iterative design cycles in the process diagram. It's not unusual for a potentially great idea to emerge late—even as late as in final development cycles. True to the notion that successive approximation is maximally open to good ideas whenever they occur (although admittedly, ideas arising very late in the process are much more difficult to deal with than ideas occurring earlier), new ideas are expected to arrive when development is underway. When this happens, a rapid prototyping cycle is initiated to think through what the ramifications are, decide what changes would have to be made, and determine whether this design should be implemented.

Not to worry. Every successive approximation plan reserves funds for problems and opportunities. You should expect and plan for at least one late arriving "bonus baby." They'll almost always feel like the most precious element conceived of within the project. They usually aren't, but they're yours! Sometimes they actually are very much "above average." It can be hard to put them in perspective at the time they have just been born, so fresh and appealing.

Be cautious however. Don't launch into full development of late-born ideas without double-checking the impact they will have on development, gathering learner reactions, and assessing the efficacy of the change or addition from the higher-level perspective of its worth to the project as a whole. For this reason, it's important to complete at least one iterative design cycle, as was done for all other designs. This can be done quickly. Really.

Prepare yourself for a surprising outcome. While the idea may prove to be just what it felt to be, other outcomes are likely. For example, it may well lead to yet another idea—perhaps one that's both better and simpler to implement. You might find that it would initiate a domino effect of changes rippling through so much completed work that it's better to omit this idea from the current project. You might find this idea appears so effective that you can actually eliminate major components of the application, whether already developed or not, saving considerable learning time and expense. You just won't know until you look carefully.

Quintuplets!

Too much of a good thing is not a good thing. Good ideas really never stop coming along. Indeed, the closer an application comes to completion, the more new ideas it seems to foster. So when bonus babies start arriving in bunches, you shouldn't conclude that you've made poor design decisions or that you haven't followed the successive approximation properly. It's the natural order of things. But don't start adopting bonus babies willy-nilly either.

It's important to realize that no application will ever be perfect, whether in its first release or its 99th. Because it's unattainable, perfection is an unaffordable and

Design Proof Evaluation Checklist

Navigation

- ❑ Is the navigation compliant with the organization's standards or consistent with other applications in use?
- ❑ Are the navigational elements recognizable and understandable?
- ❑ Are universally accepted conventions being used where appropriate?
- ❑ Does the menu effectively convey the course structure and content?
- ❑ Does the navigation provide access to required parts of the course with appropriate effort?
- ❑ If there are course resources, can the learner access them from everywhere they might be useful?
- ❑ Is it always clear to learners where they are within the application, how much they've learned, and how much remains?
- ❑ Can learners browse to look ahead or to review previous interactions?
- ❑ Are quit and resume functions working properly and available everywhere they should be?
- ❑ Are NEXT and BACK buttons working properly and available everywhere they should be?
- ◯ Are there "dead-ends"? (describe below)
- ◯ Are any helpful navigational functions missing? (describe below)

Media

- ❑ Are the representational media appealing and of appropriate quality?
- ❑ Are the representational media appropriate for this content and audience?
- ❑ Are media consistent with the organization's image and branding?
- ❑ Are media in compliance with the organization's style guide and media standards?
- ❑ Are sound effects helpful, consistent, and appropriate?
- ❑ Are any media not being displayed or presenting too slowly?
- ❑ Are media synchronized with each other on playback?
- ❑ Are media elements, including text, externalized for simplified maintenance?
- ❑ Is display space allowed for future language translation and cultural adaptation?

Interaction

- ❏ Is it always clear what options the learner has?
- ❏ Do learners know what they are supposed to do and how to respond?
- ❏ Do the interactions work properly and respond promptly?
- ❏ Are the interactions relevant?
- ❏ Are the interactions engaging?
- ❏ Can users detect and correct their own errors before they are judged?
- ❏ Are the learning activities meaningful?
- ❏ Are the learning activities appropriately challenging?
- ❏ Are the learning activities memorable?
- ❏ Are the learning activities motivational?
- ❍ How does interacting with the course make learners feel? (Are the emotional reactions appropriate and helpful?)

Content

- ❏ Does the content address targeted behaviors effectively?
- ❏ Are scenarios relevant and appropriate to learners and the learning objectives?
- ❏ Is content worded correctly and readable at an appropriate level?
- ❍ Are there content elements that need to be added or removed? (describe below)

Feedback

- ❏ Is the feedback complete and clear?
- ❏ Does the feedback make learners think?
- ❏ Does the feedback reflect the consequences of learner actions and decisions?
- ❏ Does the feedback provide additional resources for help or exploration?
- ❏ Does the feedback reinforce a change in behavior?
- ❏ If feedback is delayed, is it presented at the most effective time?

foolhardy goal. If you've done a good job adhering to the process and managing resources effectively, you will be able to assess and, if you so choose, act on one or more late arrivals. But when you've exhausted the resources you have, including the time you will need to complete validation iterations for the changes made, stop. Stop. And feel good about it.

The process will have worked, and you will have the best product you could produce, given whatever constraints you were working with. Don't start reevaluating decisions you have made. Your application may not be perfect, but you will have met the deadline, produced an excellent product, and have the basis for future iterations, should they prove to be of interest and value.

The Production Cycle and Alpha Release

Feedback from the Design Proof supplies all the information you need for finalizing any models you're building and all structures you are using. Although it's always challenging to do well, development of content is now a production-line issue. It may be possible to do many tasks concurrently. You should not fear that models and structures are going to change and require content rework.

Completion of the Alpha Release is a major milestone. A lot of work has been done to reach this point; the needs and problems identified in the Design Proof have been addressed; content and media have been fully developed and integrated; and the project is nearly finished.

The Alpha Release is intended to be complete and fully functional. The quality assurance activities integrated into the process should have led to a solid product, and hopefully did so in a surprisingly short time.

In-scope changes

There are always improvements that can be made, and it's important to realize that there will always be compelling thoughts about how to make an application better—no matter what stage of development it's in. Knowing that there will always be more good ideas on the table and that you'll encounter yet another *need,* should you make *just this one change,* perhaps you can resist the temptation.

If you have a bonus baby situation and you haven't used your contingency time and resource, it's a judgment call, of course. It's great to be able to accommodate someone's dire urge to see a particular change incorporated, and I have to admit that some last-minute changes I've made have turned out to be the best design decisions I've made. But be sure to consider all the risks and ramifications before making any changes at this point.

Some changes are entirely appropriate at this stage of development. Expected, in-scope changes that should certainly be made include content and media corrections, functional bug fixes, and minor design changes.

Alpha Release evaluation

User feedback on the Alpha Release usually comes from the same cast of players that participated in the Design Proof review and more. You'll want both the same learners who looked at the Design Proof and some additional ones who have never seen the application. If this is a blended solution, you'll want instructors to run at least a mini class using all learning events in the sequence intended. And you'll want to work with IT and/or your LMS provider, if an LMS system is to be used, to make sure communications and data exchanges are all working properly.

Managing fixes. There may be a list of known problems. While it's best if there are none, some problems may need to slip though when they are discovered only shortly before the scheduled Alpha Release date. If the problems found are not severe or "fatal" (fatal means that the application shuts down or does something dastardly, such as corrupting data), it's best to go ahead with the Alpha Release accompanied by a list of known problems. Because the Alpha Release serves the purpose of a broadly based quality check, it's likely that some other problems will be found anyway. Delaying the Alpha when only minor problems are known to exist unnecessarily slows project completion.

Evaluation environment. Sometimes, because of security concerns or the cost of launching an application on a live network, the Alpha Release is implemented only on a test network. This is poor practice, of course, as it may delay the discovery problems until there is little time to correct any significant ones. In general, the Alpha Release or a special-purpose release should be

Alpha Release Evaluation Checklist

Navigation

❏ Recheck all Design Proof navigation items.

❏ Were navigational elements modified, added, or removed as requested?

❏ Do new or modified elements function fully as designed?

❏ Do all windows (pop-ups) have close buttons?

❏ If there are learner-accessible course resources, are all of them now loaded, available, and displaying appropriately?

❏ Is the course exit or completion handled appropriately?

Media

❏ Recheck all Design Proof media items.

❏ Were media elements modified, added, or removed as requested?

❏ Are all media loading correctly and appearing in a timely manner?

❏ Are all media appealing, of appropriate quality, and suitable for the audience?

❏ Is all needed graphical or video content integrated into the application and displaying properly?

❏ Are graphics clear, readable, and understandable?

❏ Are all sounds properly synchronized?

❏ Is text free of errors? (Check for typos, spelling and grammatical errors, truncation, color, font, etc.)

❏ Is all text written at an acceptable reading level?

○ Are there any places where media should be revised to improve impact?

Interaction

- ❑ Recheck all Design Proof interaction items.
- ❑ Were interaction elements modified, added, or removed as requested?
- ❑ Are all designed interactions now present and sequenced properly?
- ❑ Do all interactions process learner responses correctly, including unusual or unexpected responses?
- ❑ If the learner reencounters an interaction, does it behave as desired?
- ❑ Are learner responses recorded properly, per design?
- ❑ Are scores computed properly, even if scored activities are interrupted and continued or restarted?

Content

- ❑ Recheck all Design Proof content items.
- ❑ Were content elements modified, added, or removed as requested?
- ❑ Are all of the instructional objectives addressed effectively by the interactions and content?
- ❑ Is the content organized logically and effectively from the learner's viewpoint?
- ❑ Are learners given adequate opportunities to evaluate their progress?
- ❑ Is sufficient practice provided?

Feedback

- ❑ Recheck all Design Proof feedback items.
- ❑ Were feedback elements modified, added, or removed as requested?
- ❑ Is all feedback clear and meaningful to the learner?
- ❑ Do all feedback boxes/windows provide clear navigation?
- ○ Is there any section or interaction that is missing feedback?

used to test network delivery and interconnection to the LMS, if one will be used. When part of a blended solution, the Alpha Release should be used as part of a class delivered with all the complementary activities and appropriate evaluation items added to the checklist for them.

The reviewers' checklist looks similar to the Design Proof, but isn't identical, of course:

The Validation Cycle and Beta Release

During the Validation Cycle, the Alpha Release is modified according to needs and problems identified in the Alpha Review. The work can range from adding practice exercises to deleting unnecessary instructions, to almost anything at all. In general, however, work at this point is restricted to making corrections rather than to creating whole new learning events or making significant structural changes.

In-scope changes

No new components should be added at this point, and changes should only be corrections to errors, such as errors introduced in making corrections and functional problems that may have arisen from the addi-

tion of content or launching from a live server.

Beta Release evaluation

The result of the Validation Cycle is the Beta Release. It is built with the intention that it is final product. Problems may still exist because any change introduces a risk that previously working components were broken as changes were made.

The Beta Release cannot be declared the final product until an evaluation determines it to be free of defects. The Beta Release is therefore ready for implementation and testing on the specified platform and declared *Gold Candidate 1*.

The Beta Release evaluation checks the same items as in the Alpha Release evaluation did. If no prior release were tested on a live server or actually interconnected to an LMS, should that be part of the delivery environment, then it's essential to add criteria as appropriate to the Beta Review, such as validating that tracking is functional.

Gold Release

It's time to celebrate! The product is ready for its full rollout, and you've completed a project in a fraction of the time it would have taken to do this with traditional processes, specification documents as deep as twenty New York cheesecakes, and enough storyboards to wallpaper Versailles.

Most importantly, you've delivered a learning solution that's great because it enables individuals and the organization to succeed at something that is very important to them. Congratulations! Well done.

Final evaluation

You're not done yet, of course. The process still holds out that final evaluation task.

The successive approximation process uses frequent reviews and evaluations throughout the process. This is to do everything possible to assure the final product meets all the many criteria it must meet to be successful. Some of the criteria are easy to state, others almost impossible. But by involving a wide range of viewpoints and working closely with learners, there's more than an excellent chance you've succeeded in developing an outstanding learning program.

Even with all the evaluation that's been conducted, there's much more that should be done after the final rollout. What's most important is to determine whether success, as originally defined and reexamined in the Savvy Start and documented in the project plan, was actually achieved. It's regrettable that so few organizations do any serious evaluation at all, including the evaluation that could substantiate a great return on their investment.

Did customer service improve? Did sales increase? Has employee retention improved? Has profitability increased? Have more of our students been admitted to college? Have our graduates found more satisfying employment?

Of course, we would also like to know whether the behavioral changes we targeted actually occurred, so that we can take credit for some of the organizational improvements. Do our learners make fewer errors? Do they make more convincing presentations?

Levels of evaluation

Kirkpatrick's four-level evaluation model is simple and has stood the test of time, having been introduced originally in 1959 and now being available in a third edition text. Each level of evaluation will help validate decisions made throughout the process.

Because our whole process should be considered iterative, it's a natural extension of the work you have done to undertake future iterations of design and development after the program has been in use for a while. The next iteration will look at the application you have produced as a prototype and perhaps the input from evaluation data as an updated set of needs.

Here's a quick summary of the evaluations, following the Kirkpatrick model:

Level 1 Evaluation: Reactions.

You have already collected an extensive amount of information on learner reactions, but you should expect learners not involved in pre-release evaluations to have a somewhat different take on the experience than those who saw themselves as part of a study. It's easy to collect this information informally by providing learners a simple means of clicking a button to send you their comments.

Level 2 Evaluation: Learning.

The challenges of this level of evaluation are much greater than you might expect and than much of today's literature reveals. Although it's hard enough to design a good posttest, there's a real problem with relying on posttests as a measure of learning. You have probably experienced the effects of courses of study that end with a final exam. Remember how, only days after the test, you had forgotten enough material that you probably couldn't have passed again? Retention tests are required to determine whether learning of any consequence has occurred. Retention tests are those tests administered some time, say six weeks or more, after the conclusion of instruction.

Level 3 Evaluation: Behavior.

Now you're looking at an indicator of great importance. Were you able to not only build the prerequisite skills needed for performance improvement, but were you and the organization able to take this learning and realize actual behavioral change.

Resource

Kirkpatrick, D. L., and Kirkpatrick, J. D. (2005). *Evaluating training programs* (3rd ed.). San Francisco: Berrett-Koehler.

Level 4 Evaluation: Results.
Of course, everyone could have been wrong in the most important assumption of all—that achieving the prescribed behavioral changes would lead to success. In business and in academia, success is defined in many different ways, yet it was some definition of success that was the reason for the learning event. That definition of success is now the ultimate measure of yours.

And that's successive approximation

You can do it. Best wishes and good luck!

MWA.

Epilog

Experience with e-learning differs greatly from one organization to another. Although the delivery costs of e-learning are much lower than those of instructor-led learning events, especially when travel is involved, the costs of any ineffective program generate the greatest losses. With ineffective instruction, everything spent is wasted, including all the time people spend in training. The cost of missed opportunities can rise to crippling levels.

Zanick Pharmaceuticals

The situation at Zanick was quite typical. Successful organizations are made up of smart people who use past experiences to guide them. They know that it's easy to turn small challenges into bureaucratic nightmares that spin out of control, but they also know that, when a project crosses multiple organizational boundaries, it's important to get support early.

e-Learning projects typically cut across many organizational boundaries of control. Projects do, indeed, fail if they don't receive broad-based support. Content must be accurate, performance change must be supported, and there must be access to computers with sufficient capabilities. These are just a few of the critical components that often fall under separate lines of managerial control. Perhaps the best way to keep control and assure success is to use a process that invites input and builds a sense of ownership among participants.

What happened at Zanick?

Well, neither CLO Emily Hayes nor Director of Security Training George Sharpe was experienced in e-learning design and development. They had good instincts about gathering information and using prototypes to test ideas, but they didn't apply a structured process to help them work effectively and efficiently. As a result, they floundered about a good deal.

Prototypes are valuable to designers in helping them conceive successful designs as long as they are careful to consider them disposable and avoid investing too much in them too soon. But the use of prototyping in successive approximation is important for additional reasons, most notable of which is the way it gets Savvy Start participants to consider and agree on the primary goals. Agreement on goals is an important first step to securing support and building an effective context for behavioral change.

George and Emily wrote up a project plan and prepared some prototypes. These were useful tools for them, but they weren't used as a tool to gather the support they needed. After putting a lot of effort into their plan and polishing up their prototypes for presentation, it looked to others that they were steamrolling an agenda. It didn't seem that George and Emily wanted input nearly as much as they wanted praise and endorsements for their program. Endorsements came, but they were offered more as tokens of accommodation. Objections were politely postponed, becoming ticking time-bombs.

The results?

Disastrous. It wasn't so much that the developer team George put together was also learning to use e-learning authoring tools for the first time on this project, although this certainly slowed things down and limited the functionality of the applications. It wasn't so much that the instructional design was weak, although it clearly would have been better if done by experienced e-learning designers. And it wasn't that the project took so long to complete, although it did overrun both schedule and budget by several multiples because of all the changes everyone insisted on each time the team thought they had finished the final release.

No, in the end, the most regrettable failure was that supervisors thought the training had little value, especially in comparison to the on-the-job training they were providing. Instead of taking advantage of the program, which could have saved Zanick a tremendous amount in training costs while also improving the readiness of their security personnel, supervisors took a stand that personal mentoring was the only way to achieve the vigilance and readiness the company needed. They set out to prove the e-learning program was a harebrained undertaking, and by doing so, they made it true. Zanick returned to their prior conclusion that e-learning wasn't for them.

Lessons learned.

With the continually increasing cost benefits of e-learning over other forms of delivery, it's almost certain that Zanick will approach e-learning again. How long they'll wait while their competitors get the upper hand is hard to say. The lessons they might have learned, and that we can fortunately learn from their experience, are:

> ➤ Rapid prototyping is more than a way for designers to determine the approach they want to take; it's also a method of gaining critical consensus and support. Conduct rapid prototyping sessions with representative participation of the learners' supervisors and key decision-makers.
> ➤ Sometimes a cold-turkey transition guarantees a defeating backlash, regardless of how successful the new approach could be. Instead of abandoning mentoring and other behavior-shaping programs they had in place, Zanick could have used a blended approach to maintain organizational support while they explored options.

> ➤ Design and development of e-learning applications is far more complex than it may look. Getting guidance from experienced designers and using experienced developers can reduce project risks, time, and costs.
> ➤ Good ideas often arise late in the design and development process. Contingency planning can accommodate a few of them without your having to exceed budget or schedule.

Wakefield Medical University

The proverb in my fortune cookie recently read, *"Genius is born of adversity; sedated by prosperity."* I thought of Robin Taylor, the training director at Wakefield Medical University, as I read it. Robin faced so many problems, not the least of which was the fear instructors had of losing their jobs if e-learning succeeded. Robin's plan was to use these very instructors to design e-learning, despite their total lack of experience. So whether deliberately as job protection or inadvertently because of inexperience, it was doubtful that the university's instructors were about to design successful e-learning.

175

What happened at Wakefield?

After freezing in her tracks and realizing that her challenges were far greater than she initially expected, Robin sought help from her university's Instructional Sciences Department. They came in to advise Robin and conduct some seminars for the instructors. They demonstrated e-learning applications that simply presented information and those that engaged learners. They provided developers from their ranks of graduate students.

The ADDIE process was abandoned in favor of an early version of successive approximation. Robin's initial budget was set aside and a Savvy Start was completed. The Savvy Start suggested that the original content wasn't a good place to start; it was too expansive and interwoven with many lab activities that were under reconsideration and likely to change. The Savvy Start identified a narrower area of learning difficulty for many students, where learning outcomes could easily be assessed in observed performance.

Perhaps the most important point of redirection came from discussions with instructors who used e-learning in a blended format. Instead of having to explain concepts and procedures over and over to each new class, instructor time was freed up by e-learning for more interesting and important interactions with students. When the instructors considered this and learned that the university's interest in e-learning really was to improve quality and also admit more students rather than decrease the instructional staff, they warmed up to the effort—eventually contributing eagerly.

The results?

Quite remarkably, Robin's first project was successful, and successive approximation got a lot of the credit. Teaching physicians were impressed by the improved ability of learners and threw their considerable influence in support of increased use of e-learning.

The university set up an internal, learning technology department that provided important industry leadership—advising many other universities and hospitals on the use of e-learning, called computer-assisted instruction (CAI) back then. Interestingly, the department was dramatically reduced some years later as many of Robin's instructors and their successors began undertaking their own application design and development projects. And then, even more recently, as the once easy-to-learn and easy-to-use authoring tools have become harder and harder to wield, an interdisciplinary team of designers and developers was reconstituted to provide collaborative support services.

Lessons learned.

Sometimes one is fortunate to have so many challenges that there's no choice but to seek help. That's what Robin had, and seek help she did. She was doubly fortunate to have found help from an experienced team that was adept in a rapid-prototyping-based process. She learned some critical lessons:

> ➤ The Savvy Start is a forum to achieve consensus on key parameters. It often leads helpfully to a tightened focus on specific behavioral outcomes and a reduction in content scope.

> ➤ Just as it makes no sense to estimate the cost to build a house before one knows on what surface it's to be built, how many rooms it will have, and what finishes it needs, it makes no sense to budget an e-learning project until there's true consensus on key parameters.

> ➤ Unless a subject-matter expert has both high levels of proficiency with development tools and is familiar with instructional paradigms that succeed through e-learning delivery, collaborating with an expert e-learning team is well advised.

Step Up Ladders

Sometimes doubters just have no chance at all. Jim Sanders, VP of Sales at Step Up Ladders, wanted to improve the effectiveness of his sales team and others in his sales channel, but he was skeptical. He'd seen a lot of computerized solutions that just made things more complicated.

Jim's skepticism about e-learning prompted him to seek proof that e-learning could lead to better performance while cutting costs. He attended a conference and learned that out-tasking was a good way for an organization inexperienced in e-learning to get a project done right. He asked around and hired a group that had a portfolio of projects done for reputable firms.

What happened at Step Up Ladders?

The outside group Jim hired was steeped in linear application of the

ADDIE process. They conducted a needs analysis and probed in hopes of determining how much money Jim was ready to spend. At first he thought he shouldn't be playing games and making his vendor guess how much he was comfortable spending. But later, Jim regretted disclosing his cost expectations, because he thought there must be a way of determining what would be the right amount to spend—an amount that would achieve the greatest return for the investment. Having disclosed his comfort zone, he was sure his vendor would place their bid about there. And he was right.

After reviewing a presentation of a project plan and budget that exceeded Jim's expected cost only marginally *(imagine that)*, Jim was intrigued by the possibility of animating the great features of his product line. He started seeing e-learning as the presentation of his product line, and that sounded helpful. Some proposed games to "make it fun to learn product features and benefits" sounded good, too.

Jim felt his project was in good hands. Knowing that he had no background in training or e-learning, he felt it was time to back out.

He had a lot of things pressing for his time, so he delegated the project to someone in customer service.

The results?

A beautiful application was developed within budget. Jim was proud of it. It looked cool, and everyone was impressed. Rollout went fine, and salespeople appreciated having product information available online. When there were questions about specific products, salespeople just referred buyers to the e-learning website.

Sales didn't increase, unfortunately. In fact, there was a slight slip in revenues that was originally chalked up to a possible market slump but were later attributed to market penetration lost to competitors. In other words, Step Up Ladders lost ground.

The problems that Jim came to understand with great clarity were many and crippling. His e-learning vendor wanted to provide something that had appeal to Jim, and they did. Unfortunately, they lost focus on providing a business solution, and so did Jim. By delegating involvement, Jim lost his opportunity to detect and correct the problem before the project was completed. And by providing storyboards rather than prototype applications, the vendor had asked Step Up Ladders to commit to solutions without the experience necessary to evaluate them.

The performance problem wasn't that sales employees didn't know the product line well; it was that they needed to improve their sales strategies. Potential buyers with questions wanted quick answers from a sales representative who cared about their business; they didn't want referral to an e-learning program. Games can make learning more interesting, but they don't correct a misalignment of problems and solutions.

Perhaps surprisingly, Jim didn't give up and abandon e-learning. He kept the product information that was a large part of the e-learning application and converted it to a fast resource for employees to use when checking on product features. To improve the performance of his sales force, Jim sought out a vendor that had demonstrated an ability to improve the sales performance of other organizations. Fortunately, this vendor used successive approximation, insisted that Jim stay involved (which he did), and provided an application that quickly taught sales-

people to practice improved sales techniques before they approached potential buyers.

Sales more than doubled for those people who took the e-learning.

Lessons learned.

Jim's determination to succeed sustained him through a painful learning experience. He has a new perspective on e-learning and on his role as a leader. What his people can do determines the potential of his organization. Previously willing to delegate decisions about training to others, Jim now insists on being involved to assure all efforts are focused on the most important needs and to provide effective learning opportunities verified in prototypes before being fully developed and delivered.

What Jim would tell you now is:

> ➤ If you care about performance outcomes, become and stay involved in the process of designing learning programs.
> ➤ Determine the cost of poor performance, the cost of opportunities currently being lost, and the gains possible through superb performance before determining

what you're willing to spend on training programs.

➤ Communicate design proposals by rapid prototyping rather than storyboards.

➤ If you don't have in-house expertise in instructional design, e-learning project management, or multimedia application development, hire it. Success is too important to risk while trying to learn everything from scratch.

➤ Use an iterative process that allows multiple opportunities to correct mistakes and improve the solution before you roll it out.

➤ Involve learners in the process of defining needs and evaluating prototypes.

Listen up!

Each of the scenarios represented in this book is based on actual experiences I've witnessed. I changed names and combined the exploits of organizations to illustrate more points in less space, but nothing here is really fictional or unusual. Nevertheless, any similarity of names and events with real organizations is purely coincidental.

Index

Academic tests, 128–129

ADDIE (Analysis, Design, Development, Implementation): alternatives to, 43–44; components of, 37–39; definition of, 40–41; disagreements over, 40–41; illustration of, 12; interpretation of, 28, 40–41; outdated nature of, 41–42; rationale for, 37; revisions to, 39–41; and today's technology, 41–42; updates to, 39–41. See also Process

Alpha Release: changes during, 164–165; evaluation of, 165–168; feedback at, 165; key factors in, 77; rationale for, 164

Analysis: budget for, 13; typical weaknesses of, 36, 37

Assessment: defining before design learning events, 130; purpose of, 129; stipulation of, 129–131. See also Evaluation

Asynchronous learning, xiv

Authorware™, 120

Backgrounding: analysis of collected data in, 54–58; definition of, 45; key factors in, 74; online resource for, 54; purpose of, 45–46; questions for, 46–58; in Savvy Start, 90–91

Behavioral change: and backgrounding questions, 48–49, 54–56; and evaluations, 170; and incentives, 50, 56; in kickoff discussions, 102–103; in organizations, 84; and process, 35–36; requirements for, 149

Beta Release: corrections after, 155; key factors in, 77; overview of, 168

Blended learning, xvi

Boredom, 33–34

Brainstorming: in iterative design phase, 108–110, 112–113, 142; rules for, 90

Budget: backgrounding questions regarding, 51–52; dangerous assumptions regarding, 22; and iterative phase discussion, 136, 139–140; optimization of, 66–67; problems with, 12–14; in training program sample, 64; uneasiness about, 60–61

Budget makers, 25

Candidate learners, 25

Carliner, S., 41

Checklists: for Alpha Release evaluation, 166–167; for Design Proof evaluation, 162–163; for quality assurance, 78–79

Clark, D., 38, 40

About Allen Interactions Inc.

Allen Interactions was formed by learning technology pioneers who have continuously created precedent-setting learning solutions since the late 1960s. Their award-winning custom design and development services have been commissioned by Apple Computer, American Express, Bank of America, Boston Scientific, Delta Air Lines, Ecolab, IBM, Medtronic, Merck, Motorola, Nextel, UPS, and hundreds of other leading corporations.

Working with IBM and then with Control Data Corporation, Michael Allen led the development of the first two widely used LMS systems. His pioneering work on visual authoring systems led to the ground-breaking introduction of Authorware, elevated the level of interactivity that educators could develop, and launched Macromedia, together with a new industry of interactive multimedia tools.

Now, his studios at Allen Interactions carry on the search for more meaningful, memorable, and motivational instructional paradigms, faster and lower-cost methods of designing and building technology-enhanced learning solutions, and ways to share their discoveries with those interested in more effective learning.

About the Author

Starting his work in technology-enhanced learning at Cornell College in the late 1960s, he has been developing instructional paradigms, systems, and innovative tools ever since. Michael W. Allen holds M.A. and Ph.D. degrees in educational psychology from The Ohio State University. He is an adjunct associate professor at the University of Minnesota Medical School in the Department of Family Medicine and Community Health.

Active in e-learning organizations, publishing, and speaking, he has consulted internationally with governments and major corporations on the use of technology for learning. Dr. Allen created the first commercial LMS products used internationally, the precedent-setting visual authoring tool, Authorware, and countless instructional applications. His first book, Michael Allen's Guide to e-Learning: Building interactive, fun, and effective learning programs for any company, has been praised by beginners and experts alike. Dr. Allen's advice is based on unrivaled experience and insights.

About Pfeiffer

Pfeiffer serves the professional development and hands-on resource needs of training and human resource practitioners and gives them products to do their jobs better. We deliver proven ideas and solutions from experts in HR development and HR management, and we offer effective and customizable tools to improve workplace performance. From novice to seasoned professional, Pfeiffer is the source you can trust to make yourself and your organization more successful.

Essential Knowledge Pfeiffer produces insightful, practical, and comprehensive materials on topics that matter the most to training and HR professionals. Our Essential Knowledge resources translate the expertise of seasoned professionals into practical, how-to guidance on critical workplace issues and problems. These resources are supported by case studies, worksheets, and job aids and are frequently supplemented with CD-ROMs, websites, and other means of making the content easier to read, understand, and use.

Essential Tools Pfeiffer's Essential Tools resources save time and expense by offering proven, ready-to-use materials—including exercises, activities, games, instruments, and assessments—for use during a training or team-learning event. These resources are frequently offered in looseleaf or CD-ROM format to facilitate copying and customization of the material.

Pfeiffer also recognizes the remarkable power of new technologies in expanding the reach and effectiveness of training. While e-hype has often created whizbang solutions in search of a problem, we are dedicated to bringing convenience and enhancements to proven training solutions. All our e-tools comply with rigorous functionality standards. The most appropriate technology wrapped around essential content yields the perfect solution for today's on-the-go trainers and human resource professionals.

Pfeiffer
www.pfeiffer.com

Essential resources for training and HR professionals

Pfeiffer Publications Guide

This guide is designed to familiarize you with the various types of Pfeiffer publications. The formats section describes the various types of products that we publish; the methodologies section describes the many different ways that content might be provided within a product. We also provide a list of the topic areas in which we publish.

FORMATS

In addition to its extensive book-publishing program, Pfeiffer offers content in an array of formats, from fieldbooks for the practitioner to complete, ready-to-use training packages that support group learning.

FIELDBOOK Designed to provide information and guidance to practitioners in the midst of action. Most fieldbooks are companions to another, sometimes earlier, work, from which its ideas are derived; the fieldbook makes practical what was theoretical in the original text. Fieldbooks can certainly be read from cover to cover. More likely, though, you'll find yourself bouncing around following a particular theme, or dipping in as the mood, and the situation, dictate.

HANDBOOK A contributed volume of work on a single topic, comprising an eclectic mix of ideas, case studies, and best practices sourced by practitioners and experts in the field.

An editor or team of editors usually is appointed to seek out contributors and to evaluate content for relevance to the topic. Think of a handbook not as a ready-to-eat meal, but as a cookbook of ingredients that enables you to create the most fitting experience for the occasion.

RESOURCE Materials designed to support group learning. They come in many forms: a complete, ready-to-use exercise (such as a game); a comprehensive resource on one topic (such as conflict management) containing a variety of methods and approaches; or a collection of like-minded activities (such as icebreakers) on multiple subjects and situations.

TRAINING PACKAGE An entire, ready-to-use learning program that focuses on a particular topic or skill. All packages comprise a guide for the facilitator/trainer and a workbook for the participants. Some packages are supported with additional media—such as video—or learning aids, instruments, or other devices to help participants understand concepts or practice and develop skills.

- *Facilitator/trainer's guide* Contains an introduction to the program, advice on how to organize and facilitate the learning event, and step-by-step instructor notes. The guide also contains copies of presentation materials—handouts, presentations, and overhead designs, for example—used in the program.

• *Participant's workbook* Contains exercises and reading materials that support the learning goal and serves as a valuable reference and support guide for participants in the weeks and months that follow the learning event. Typically, each participant will require his or her own workbook.

ELECTRONIC CD-ROMs and web-based products transform static Pfeiffer content into dynamic, interactive experiences. Designed to take advantage of the searchability, automation, and ease-of-use that technology provides, our e-products bring convenience and immediate accessibility to your workspace.

METHODOLOGIES

CASE STUDY A presentation, in narrative form, of an actual event that has occurred inside an organization. Case studies are not prescriptive, nor are they used to prove a point; they are designed to develop critical analysis and decision-making skills. A case study has a specific time frame, specifies a sequence of events, is narrative in structure, and contains a plot structure—an issue (what should be/have been done?). Use case studies when the goal is to enable participants to apply previously learned theories to the circumstances in the case, decide what is pertinent, identify the real issues, decide what should have been done, and develop a plan of action.

ENERGIZER A short activity that develops readiness for the next session or learning event. Energizers are most commonly used after a break or lunch to stimulate or refocus the group. Many involve some form of physical activity, so they are a useful way to counter post-lunch lethargy. Other uses include transitioning from one topic to another, where "mental" distancing is important.

EXPERIENTIAL LEARNING ACTIVITY (ELA) A facilitator-led intervention that moves participants through the learning cycle from experience to application (also known as a Structured Experience). ELAs are carefully thought-out designs in which there is a definite learning purpose and intended outcome. Each step—everything that participants do during the activity—facilitates the accomplishment of the stated goal. Each ELA includes complete instructions for facilitating the intervention and a clear statement of goals, suggested group size and timing, materials required, an explanation of the process, and, where appropriate, possible variations to the activity. (For more detail on Experiential Learning Activities, see the Introduction to the *Reference Guide to Handbooks and Annuals*, 1999 edition, Pfeiffer, San Francisco.)

GAME A group activity that has the purpose of fostering team spirit and togetherness in addition to the achievement of a pre-stated goal. Usually contrived—undertaking a desert expedition, for example—this type of learning method offers an engaging means for participants to demonstrate and practice business and interpersonal skills. Games are effective for team building and personal development mainly because the goal is subordinate to the process—the means through which participants reach decisions, collaborate, communicate, and generate trust and understanding. Games often engage teams in "friendly" competition.

ICEBREAKER A (usually) short activity designed to help participants overcome initial anxiety in a training session and/or to acquaint the participants with one another. An icebreaker can be a fun activity or can be tied to specific topics or training goals. While a useful tool in itself, the icebreaker comes into its own in situations where tension or resistance exists within a group.

INSTRUMENT A device used to assess, appraise, evaluate, describe, classify, and summarize various aspects of human behavior. The term used to describe an instrument depends primarily on its format and purpose. These terms include survey, questionnaire, inventory, diagnostic, survey, and poll. Some uses of instruments include providing instrumental feedback to group members, studying here-and-now processes or functioning within a group, manipulating group composition, and evaluating outcomes of training and other interventions.

Instruments are popular in the training and HR field because, in general, more growth can occur if an individual is provided with a method for focusing specifically on his or her own behavior. Instruments also are used to obtain information that will serve as a basis for change and to assist in workforce planning efforts.

Paper-and-pencil tests still dominate the instrument landscape with a typical package comprising a facilitator's guide, which offers advice on administering the instrument and interpreting the collected data, and an initial set of instruments. Additional instruments are available separately. Pfeiffer, though, is investing heavily in e-instruments. Electronic instrumentation provides effortless distribution and, for larger groups particularly, offers advantages over paper-and-pencil tests in the time it takes to analyze data and provide feedback.

LECTURETTE A short talk that provides an explanation of a principle, model, or process that is pertinent to the participants' current learning needs. A lecturette is intended to establish a common language bond between the trainer and the participants by providing a mutual frame of reference. Use a lecturette as an introduction to a group activity or event, as an interjection during an event, or as a handout.

MODEL A graphic depiction of a system or process and the relationship among its elements. Models provide a frame of reference and something more tangible, and more easily remembered, than a verbal explanation. They also give participants something to "go on," enabling them to track their own progress as they experience the dynamics, processes, and relationships being depicted in the model.

ROLE PLAY A technique in which people assume a role in a situation/scenario: a customer service rep in an angry-customer exchange, for example. The way in which the role is approached is then discussed and feedback is offered. The role play is often repeated using a different approach and/or incorporating changes made based on feedback received. In other words, role playing is a spontaneous interaction involving realistic behavior under artificial (and safe) conditions.

SIMULATION A methodology for understanding the interrelationships among components of a system or process. Simulations differ from games in that they test or use a model that depicts or mirrors some aspect of reality in form, if not necessarily in content. Learning occurs by studying the effects of change on one or more factors of the model. Simulations are commonly used to test hypotheses about what happens in a system—often referred to as "what if?" analysis—or to examine best-case/worst-case scenarios.

THEORY A presentation of an idea from a conjectural perspective. Theories are useful because they encourage us to examine behavior and phenomena through a different lens.

TOPICS

The twin goals of providing effective and practical solutions for workforce training and organization development and meeting the educational needs of training and human resource professionals shape Pfeiffer's publishing program. Core topics include the following:

Leadership & Management

Communication & Presentation

Coaching & Mentoring

Training & Development

E-Learning

Teams & Collaboration

OD & Strategic Planning

Human Resources

Consulting

What will you find on pfeiffer.com?

- The best in workplace performance solutions for training and HR professionals

- Downloadable training tools, exercises, and content

- Web-exclusive offers

- Training tips, articles, and news

- Seamless on-line ordering

- Author guidelines, information on becoming a Pfeiffer Affiliate, and much more

Discover more at www.pfeiffer.com

Customer Care

Have a question, comment, or suggestion? Contact us! We value your feedback and we want to hear from you.

For questions about this or other Pfeiffer products, you may contact us by:

E-mail: **customer@wiley.com**

Mail:　**Customer Care Wiley/Pfeiffer**
　　　　10475 Crosspoint Blvd.
　　　　Indianapolis, IN 46256

Phone: **(US) 800-274-4434** (Outside the US: 317-572-3985)

Fax:　 **(US) 800-569-0443** (Outside the US: 317-572-4002)

To order additional copies of this title or to browse other Pfeiffer products, visit us online at **www.pfeiffer.com**.

For **Technical Support** questions call **(800) 274-4434**.

For authors guidelines, log on to www.pfeiffer.com and click on "Resources for Authors."

If you are . . .

A **college bookstore, a professor, an instructor, or work in higher education** and you'd like to place an order or request an exam copy, please contact jbreview@wiley.com.

A **general retail bookseller** and you'd like to establish an account or speak to a local sales representative, contact Melissa Grecco at 201-748-6267 or mgrecco@wiley.com.

An **exclusively on-line bookseller**, contact Amy Blanchard at 530-756-9456 or ablanchard @wiley.com or Jennifer Johnson at 206-568-3883 or jjohnson@wiley.com, both of our Online Sales department.

A **librarian or library representative**, contact John Chambers in our Library Sales department at 201-748-6291 or jchamber@wiley.com.

A **reseller, training company/consultant, or corporate trainer**, contact Charles Regan in our Special Sales department at 201-748-6553 or cregan@wiley.com.

A **specialty retail distributor** (includes specialty gift stores, museum shops, and corporate bulk sales), contact Kim Hendrickson in our Special Sales department at 201-748-6037 or khendric@wiley.com.

Purchasing for the **Federal government**, contact Ron Cunningham in our Special Sales department at 317-572-3053 or rcunning@wiley.com.

Purchasing for a **State or Local government**, contact Charles Regan in our Special Sales department at 201-748-6553 or cregan@wiley.com.